THE MYSTERY OF CAPITAL

THE MYSTERY OF CAPITAL

WHY CAPITALISM TRIUMPHS IN THE WEST AND FAILS EVERYWHERE ELSE

Hernando de Soto

BANTAM PRESS

LONDON · NEW YORK · TORONTO · SYDNEY · AUCKLAND

TRANSWORLD PUBLISHERS
61–63 Uxbridge Road, London W5 5SA
a division of The Random House Group Ltd

RANDOM HOUSE AUSTRALIA (PTY) LTD
20 Alfred Street, Milsons Point, Sydney
New South Wales 2061, Australia

RANDOM HOUSE NEW ZEALAND
18 Poland Road, Glenfield, Auckland 10, New Zealand

RANDOM HOUSE SOUTH AFRICA (PTY) LTD
Endulini, 5a Jubilee Road, Parktown 2193, South Africa

Published 2000 by Bantam Press
a division of Transworld Publishers

A catalogue record for this book is available
from the British Library
ISBN 0593 046641

Typeset in 10½/14pt Sabon by Falcon Oast Graphic Art

Printed in Great Britain
by Clays Ltd, St Ives plc

1 3 5 7 9 10 8 6 4 2

To Mariano Cornejo, who showed me how to stand firmly on the ground, and to Duncan Macdonald, who taught me how to navigate by the stars.

CONTENTS

1

THE FIVE MYSTERIES OF CAPITAL

The key problem is to find out why that sector of society of the past, which I would not hesitate to call capitalist, should have lived as if in a bell jar, cut off from the rest; why was it not able to expand and conquer the whole of society? . . . [Why was it that] a significant rate of capital formation was possible only in certain sectors and not in the whole market economy of the time?

FERNAND BRAUDEL, The Wheels of Commerce

The hour of capitalism's greatest triumph is its hour of crisis.

The fall of the Berlin Wall ended more than a century of political competition between capitalism and communism. Capitalism stands alone as the only feasible way rationally to organize a modern economy. At this moment in history, no responsible nation has a choice. As a result, with varying degrees of enthusiasm, Third World and former communist nations have balanced their budgets, cut subsidies, welcomed foreign investment and dropped their tariff barriers.

Their efforts have been repaid with bitter disappointment. From Russia to Venezuela, the past half-decade has been a time of economic suffering, tumbling incomes, anxiety and resentment; of 'starving, rioting and looting', in the stinging words of Malaysian Prime Minister Mahathir Mohamad. In a recent editorial the *New York Times* said: 'For much of the world, the marketplace extolled by the West in the afterglow of victory in the Cold War has been supplanted by the cruelty of markets, wariness towards capitalism and dangers of instability.' The triumph of capitalism only in the West could be a recipe for economic and political disaster.

For Americans enjoying both peace and prosperity, it has been all too easy to ignore the turmoil elsewhere. How can capitalism be in trouble when the Dow Jones Industrial average is climbing higher than Sir Edmund Hillary? Americans look at other nations and see progress, even if it is slow and uneven. Can't you eat a Big Mac in Moscow, rent a Blockbuster video in Shanghai, and reach the Internet in Caracas?

Even in the United States, however, the foreboding cannot be completely stifled. Americans see Colombia poised on the brink of a major civil war between drug-trafficking guerrillas and repressive militias; an intractable insurgency in the south of Mexico; an important part of Asia's force-fed economic growth draining away into corruption and chaos. In Latin America sympathy for free markets is dwindling: concretely, by May 2000 support for privatization had dropped from 46 per cent of the population to 36 per cent. Most ominously of all, in the former communist nations capitalism has been found wanting, and men associated with old regimes stand poised to resume power. Some Americans sense, too, that one reason for their decade-long boom is that the more precarious the rest of the world looks, the more attractive American stocks and bonds become as a haven for international money.

In the business community of the West there is a growing concern that the failure of most of the rest of the world to implement capitalism will eventually drive the rich economies into recession. As millions of investors have painfully learned from the evaporation of their emerging market funds, globalization is a two-way street: if the Third World and former communist nations cannot escape the influence of the West, nor can the West disentangle itself from them. Adverse reactions to capitalism have also been growing stronger within rich countries themselves. The rioting both in Seattle at the meeting of the World Trade Organization in December 1999 and a few months later at the IMF/World Bank meeting in Washington, DC, regardless of the diversity of the grievances, highlighted the anger that spreading capitalism inspires. Many have begun recalling the economic historian Karl Polanyi's warnings that free markets can collide with society and lead to fascism. Japan is struggling through its most prolonged slump since the Great Depression. Western Europeans vote for politicians who promise them a 'third way' that rejects what a French bestseller has labelled *L'horreur économique*.

These whispers of alarm, disturbing though they are, have thus far only prompted American and European leaders to repeat to the rest of the world the same wearisome lectures: stabilize your currencies, hang tough, ignore the food riots, and wait patiently for the foreign investors to return.

Foreign investment is, of course, a very good thing. The more of it, the better. Stable currencies are good, too, as are free trade and transparent banking practices and the privatization of state-owned industries and every other remedy in the Western pharmacopoeia. Yet we continually forget that global capitalism has been tried before. In Latin America, for example, reforms directed at creating capitalist systems have been tried at least four times since independence from Spain in the 1820s. Each time, after the initial euphoria, Latin Americans swung back from capitalist and market economy policies. These remedies are clearly not enough. Indeed, they fall so far short as to be almost irrelevant.

When these remedies fail, Westerners all too often respond not by questioning the adequacy of the remedies but by blaming Third World peoples for their lack of entrepreneurial spirit or market orientation. If they have failed to prosper despite all the excellent advice, it is because something is the matter with them: they missed the Protestant Reformation, or they are crippled by the disabling legacy of colonial Europe, or their IQs are too low. But the suggestion that it is culture that explains the success of such diverse places as Japan, Switzerland and California, and culture again that explains the relative poverty of such equally diverse places as China, Estonia and Baja California, is worse than inhumane: it is unconvincing. The disparity of wealth between the West and the rest of the world is far too big to be explained by culture alone. Most people want the fruits of capital, so much so that many, from the children of Sanchez to Khrushchev's son, are flocking to Western nations.

The cities of the Third World and the former communist countries are teeming with entrepreneurs. You cannot walk through a Middle Eastern market, hike up to a Latin American village or climb into a taxi in Moscow without someone trying to make a deal with you. The inhabitants of these countries possess talent, enthusiasm and an astonishing ability to wring a profit out of practically nothing. They can grasp and use modern technology. Otherwise, American businesses would not be struggling to control the unauthorized use of their patents abroad; nor would the US government be striving so desperately to keep modern weapons technology out of the hands of Third World countries. Markets are an ancient and universal tradition: Christ drove the merchants out of the temple 2,000 years ago, and Mexicans were taking their products to market long before Columbus reached America.

But if people in countries making the transition to capitalism are not pitiful beggars, are not helplessly trapped in obsolete ways, and are not the uncritical prisoners of dysfunctional cultures, what is it that prevents capitalism from delivering to them the same wealth it has delivered to the West? Why does capitalism thrive only in the West, as if enclosed in a bell jar?

In this book I intend to demonstrate that the major stumbling block that keeps the rest of the world from benefiting from capitalism is its inability to produce capital. Capital is the force that raises the productivity of labour and creates the wealth of nations. It is the lifeblood of the capitalist system, the foundation of progress, and the one thing that the poor countries of the world cannot seem to produce for themselves, no matter how eagerly their peoples engage in all the other activities that characterize a capitalist economy.

I will also show, with the help of facts and figures that my research team and I have collected, block by block and farm by farm in Asia, Africa, the Middle East and Latin America, that most of the poor already possess the assets they need to make a success of capitalism. Even in the poorest countries the poor save. The value of savings among the poor is, in fact, immense: forty times all the foreign aid received throughout the world since 1945. In Egypt, for instance, the wealth that the poor have accumulated is worth fifty-five times as much as the sum of all direct foreign investment ever recorded there, including the Suez Canal and the Aswan Dam.

In Haiti, the poorest nation in Latin America, the total assets of the poor are more than 150 times greater than all the foreign investment received since the country's independence from France in 1804. If the United States were to hike its foreign-aid budget to the level recommended by the United Nations – 0.7 per cent of national income – it would take the richest country on earth more than 150 years to transfer to the world's poor resources equal to those that they already possess.

But they hold these resources in defective forms: houses built on land whose ownership rights are not adequately recorded, unincorporated businesses with undefined liability, industries located where financiers and investors cannot see them. Because the rights to these possessions are not adequately documented, these assets cannot readily be turned into capital, cannot be traded outside of narrow local circles where people know and trust each other, cannot be used as collateral for a loan and cannot be used as a share against an investment.

In the West, by contrast, every parcel of land, every building, every piece of equipment or store of inventories is represented in a property document that is the visible sign of a vast hidden process that connects all these assets to the rest of the economy. Thanks to this representational process, assets can lead an invisible, parallel life alongside their material existence. They can be used as collateral for credit. The single most important source of funds for new businesses in the United States is a mortgage on the entrepreneur's house. These assets can also provide a link to the owner's credit history, an accountable address for the collection of debts and taxes, the basis for the creation of reliable and universal public utilities, and a foundation for the creation of securities (like mortgage-backed bonds) that can then be rediscounted and sold in secondary markets. By this process the West injects life into assets and makes them generate capital.

Third World and former communist nations do not have this representational process. As a result, most of them are undercapitalized, in the same way that a firm is undercapitalized when it issues fewer securities than its income and assets would justify. The enterprises of the poor are very much like corporations that cannot issue shares or bonds to obtain new investment and finance. Without representations, their assets are dead capital.

The poor inhabitants of these nations – the overwhelming majority – do have things, but they lack the process to represent their property and create capital. They have houses but not titles; crops but not deeds; businesses but not statutes of incorporation. It is the unavailability of these essential representations that explains why people who have adapted every other Western invention, from the paper clip to the nuclear reactor, have not been able to produce sufficient capital to make their domestic capitalism work.

This is the mystery of capital. Solving it requires an understanding of why Westerners, by representing assets with titles, are able to see and draw out capital from them. One of the greatest challenges to the human mind is to comprehend and gain access to those things we know exist but cannot see. Not everything that is real and useful is tangible and visible. Time, for example, is real, but it can only be efficiently managed when it is represented by a clock or a calendar. Throughout history, human beings have invented representational systems – writing, musical notation, double-entry bookkeeping – to grasp with the mind what human hands could never touch. In the same way the great practitioners of capitalism, from the creators of integrated title systems and corporate stock to Michael Milken, were able to reveal and extract capital where others saw just junk by devising new ways to represent the invisible potential that is locked into the assets we accumulate.

At this very moment you are surrounded by waves of Ukrainian, Chinese and Brazilian television that you cannot see. So, too, are you surrounded by assets that invisibly harbour capital. Just as the waves of Ukrainian television are far too weak for you to sense them directly but can, with the help of a TV, be decoded to be seen and heard, so can capital be extracted and processed from assets. But only the West has the conversion process required to transform the invisible to the visible. It is this disparity that explains why Western nations can create capital and the Third World and former communist nations cannot.

The absence of this process, in the poorer regions of the world where five-sixths of humanity live, is not the consequence of some Western monopolistic conspiracy. It is rather that Westerners take this mechanism so completely for granted that they have lost all awareness of its existence. Although it is huge, nobody sees it, including the Americans, Europeans and Japanese who owe all their wealth to their ability to use it. It is an implicit legal infrastructure hidden deep within their property systems – of which ownership is but the tip of the iceberg. The rest of the iceberg is an intricate man-made process that can transform assets and labour into capital. This process was not created from a blueprint and is not described in a glossy brochure. Its origins are obscure and its significance buried in the economic subconscious of Western capitalist nations.

How could something so important have slipped our minds? It is not uncommon for us to know *how* to use things without understanding why they work. Sailors used magnetic compasses long before there was a satisfactory theory of magnetism. Animal breeders had a working knowledge of genetics long before Gregor Mendel explained genetic principles. Even as the West prospers from abundant capital, do people really understand the origin of that capital? If they don't, there always remains the possibility that the West might damage the source of its own strength. Being clear about the source of capital will also prepare the West to protect itself and the rest of the world as soon as the prosperity of the moment yields to the crisis that is sure to come. Then the question that always arises in international crises will be heard again: 'Whose money will be used to solve the problem?'

So far, Western countries have been happy to take their system for producing capital entirely for granted and to leave its history undocumented. That history must be recovered. This book is an effort to reopen the exploration of the source of capital and thus explain how to correct the economic failures of poor countries. These failures have nothing to do with deficiencies in cultural or genetic heritage. Would anyone suggest 'cultural' commonalities between Latin Americans and Russians? Yet in the last decade, ever since both regions began to build capitalism without capital, they have shared the same political, social and economic problems: glaring inequality, underground economies, pervasive mafias, political instability, capital flight, flagrant disregard for the law. These troubles did not originate in the monasteries of the Orthodox Church or along the pathways of the Incas.

But it is not only ex-communist and Third World countries that have suffered all of these problems. The same was true of the United States in 1783, when President George Washington complained about 'banditti . . . skimming and disposing of the cream of the country at the expense of the many'. These 'banditti' were squatters and small illegal entrepreneurs occupying lands they did not own. For the next hundred years, such squatters battled for legal rights to their land and miners warred over their claims because ownership laws differed from town to town and camp to camp. Enforcing property rights created such a quagmire of social unrest and antagonism throughout the young United States that the Chief Justice of the Supreme Court, Joseph Story, wondered in 1820 whether lawyers would ever be able to settle them.

Do squatters, bandits and flagrant disregard of the law sound familiar? Americans and Europeans have been telling the other countries of the world, 'You have to be more like us.' In fact, they are very much like the United States of a century ago, when it, too, was a Third World country. Western politicians once faced the same dramatic challenges that leaders of the developing and former communist countries are facing today. But their successors have lost contact with the days when the pioneers who opened the American West were undercapitalized because they seldom possessed title to the lands they settled and the goods they owned; when Adam Smith did his shopping in black markets and English street urchins plucked pennies cast by laughing tourists into the mud banks of the Thames; when Jean-Baptiste Colbert's technocrats executed 16,000 small entrepreneurs whose only crime was manufacturing and importing cotton cloth in violation of France's industrial codes.

That past is many nations' present. The Western nations have so successfully integrated their poor into their economies that they have lost even the memory of how it was done, how the creation of capital began back when, as the American historian Gordon Wood has written, 'something momentous was happening in the society and culture that released the aspirations and energies of common people as never before in American history.'[1] The 'something momentous' was that

Americans and Europeans were on the verge of establishing widespread formal property law and inventing the conversion process in that law that allowed them to create capital. This was the moment when the West crossed the demarcation line that led to successful capitalism – when it ceased being a private club and became a popular culture, when George Washington's dreaded 'banditti' were transformed into the beloved pioneers that American culture now venerates.

The paradox is as clear as it is unsettling: capital, the most essential component of Western economic advance, is the one that has received the least attention. Neglect has shrouded it in mystery – in fact, in a series of five mysteries.

Δ **The Mystery of Missing Information**
Charitable organizations have so emphasized the miseries and helplessness of the world's poor that no one has properly documented their capacity for accumulating assets. Over the past five years, I and a hundred colleagues from six different nations have closed our books and opened our eyes – and gone out into the streets and countrysides of four continents to count how much the poorest sectors of society have saved. The quantity is enormous. But most of it is dead capital.

Δ **The Mystery of Capital**
This is the key mystery and the centrepiece of this book. Capital is a subject that has fascinated thinkers for the last three centuries: Marx said that you needed to go beyond physics to touch 'the hen that lays the golden eggs'; Adam Smith felt you had to create 'a sort of waggon-way through the air' to reach that same hen. But no one has told us where the hen hides. What is capital, how is it produced, and how is it related to money?

Δ **The Mystery of Political Awareness**
If there is so much dead capital in the world, and in the hands of so many poor people, why haven't governments tried to tap into this potential wealth? Simply because the evidence they needed

has only become available in the past forty years as billions of people throughout the world have moved from life organized on a small scale to life on a large scale. This migration to the cities has rapidly divided labour and spawned in poorer countries a huge industrial/commercial revolution – one that, incredibly, has been virtually ignored.

Δ **The Missing Lessons of US History**
What is going on in the Third World and the ex-communist countries has happened before, in Europe and North America. Unfortunately, we have been so mesmerized by the failure of so many nations to make the transition to capitalism that we have forgotten how the successful capitalist nations did it. For years, I visited technocrats and politicians in advanced nations, from Alaska to Tokyo, but they had no answers. It was a mystery. I finally found the answer in their history books, the most pertinent example being that of US history.

Δ **The Mystery of Legal Failure: Why Property Law Does Not Work Outside the West**
Since the nineteenth century, nations have been copying the laws of the West to give their citizens the institutional framework to produce wealth. They continue to copy such laws today, and, obviously, it doesn't work. Most citizens still cannot use the law to convert their savings into capital. Why this is so and what is needed to make the law work remains a mystery.

The solution to each of these mysteries will be the subject of a chapter in this book.

The moment is ripe to solve the problems of why capitalism is triumphant in the West and stalling practically everywhere else. As all plausible alternatives to capitalism have now evaporated, we are finally in a position to study capital dispassionately and carefully.

2

THE MYSTERY OF MISSING INFORMATION

*Economics, over the years, has become more and more abstract
and divorced from events in the real world. Economists, by and
large, do not study the workings of the actual economic system.
They theorize about it. As Ely Devons, an English economist,
once said at a meeting, 'If economists wished to study the horse,
they wouldn't go and look at horses. They'd sit in their studies
and say to themselves, "What would I do if I were a horse?"'*

RONALD H. COASE, *The Task of the Society*

Imagine a country where nobody can identify who owns what,
addresses cannot be easily verified, people cannot be made to
pay their debts, resources cannot conveniently be turned into
money, ownership cannot be divided into shares, descriptions
of assets are not standardized and cannot be easily compared,
and the rules that govern property vary from neighbourhood
to neighbourhood or even from street to street. You have just
put yourself into the life of a developing country or former
communist nation; more precisely, you have imagined life for
80 per cent of its population, which is marked off as sharply
from its Westernized élite as black and white South Africans
were once separated by apartheid.

This 80 per cent majority is not, as Westerners often

imagine, desperately impoverished. In spite of their obvious poverty, even those who live under the most grossly unequal regimes possess far more than anybody has ever understood. What they possess, however, is not represented in such a way as to produce additional value. When you step out the door of the Nile Hilton, what you are leaving behind is not the high-technology world of fax machines and icemakers, television and antibiotics. The people of Cairo have access to all those things. What you are really leaving behind is the world of legally enforceable transactions on property rights. Mortgages and accountable addresses to generate additional wealth are unavailable even to those people in Cairo who would probably strike you as quite rich. Outside Cairo, some of the poorest of the poor live in a district of old tombs called 'the city of the dead'. But almost all of Cairo is a city of the dead – of dead capital, of assets that cannot be used to their fullest. The institutions that give life to capital – that allow you to secure the interests of third parties with your work and assets – do not exist here.

To understand how this is possible, one must look to the nineteenth century, when the United States was carving a society out of its own wilderness. The United States had inherited from Britain not only its fantastically complex land law but a vast system of overlapping land grants. The same acre might belong to one man who had received it as part of a vast land grant from the British Crown, to another who claimed to have bought it from an Indian tribe and to a third who had accepted it in place of salary from a state legislature – and none of the three might ever have laid eyes on it. Meanwhile, the country was filling up with immigrants, who settled boundaries, ploughed fields, built homes, transferred land and established credit long before governments conferred on them any right to engage in these acts. Those were the days of the pioneers and the 'Wild West'. One of the reasons it was so wild was that those pioneers, most of them nothing but squatters, 'insisted that their labor, not formal paper titles or arbitrary boundary lines, gave land value and established ownership'.[1] They believed that if they occupied the land and improved it with houses and farms, it was theirs. State and federal governments believed otherwise. Officials sent in troops to burn farms and destroy buildings. Settlers fought back. When the soldiers left, the settlers rebuilt and returned to scratching out a living. That past is the Third World's present.

A Surprise Revolution

Before 1950, most Third World countries were agricultural societies organized in ways that would have made an eighteenth-century European feel right at home. Most people worked on the land, which was owned by a very few big land-lords, some of them indigenous oligarchs, others colonial planters. Cities were small and functioned as markets and ports rather than industrial centres; they were dominated by tiny mercantile élites who protected their interests with thick wrappings of rules and regulations.

After 1950, there began in the Third World an economic revolution similar to the social and economic disruptions in Europe in 1800. New machines were reducing the demand for rural labour just as new medicines and public-health methods were cutting the rate of infant mortality and extending life-spans. Soon hundreds of thousands of people were trundling down the newly built highways to the cities so alluringly described in the new radio programmes.

The population of the cities began to rise rapidly. In China alone more than 100 million people have moved from the countryside to the cities since 1979. Between 1950 and 1988 the population of metropolitan Port-au-Prince rose from 140,000 to 1,550,000. By 1998, it was approaching 2 million. Almost two-thirds of these people live in shanty towns. Experts were already in despair over this surge of new city dwellers as early as 1973, long before the largest influx had taken place. 'Everything happens as if the city were falling apart,' wrote one urbanist. 'Uncontrolled construction, any- where anyhow. The sewage system is incapable of helping drain rainwater and stuffs up every day. The population con- centrates in defined areas where no sanitation infrastructure is provided. The sidewalks of the Avenue Dessalines are literally occupied by small vendors. This town has become unlivable.'[2]

Few had anticipated this enormous transformation in the way people lived and worked. The fashionable theories of the day about 'development' sought to bring modernity to the countryside. Peasants were not supposed to come to the cities looking for the twentieth century. But tens of millions came anyway, despite a backlash of mounting hostility. They faced an impenetrable wall of rules that barred them from legally established social and economic activities. It was tremendously difficult for these new city people to acquire legal housing, enter formal business or find a legal job.

The Obstacles to Legality

To get an idea of just how difficult the migrant's life was, my research team and I opened a small garment workshop on the outskirts of Lima. Our goal was to create a new and perfectly legal business. The team then began filling out the forms, standing in the queues and making the bus trips into central Lima to get all the certifications required to operate, according to the letter of the law, a small business in Peru. They spent six hours a day at it and finally registered the business – 289 days later. Although the garment workshop was geared to operating with only one worker, the cost of legal registration was $1,231 – thirty-one times the monthly minimum wage. To obtain legal authorization to build a house on state-owned land took six years and eleven months – requiring 207 administrative steps in 52 government offices (see Figure 2.1). To obtain a legal title for that piece of land it took 728 steps. We also found that a

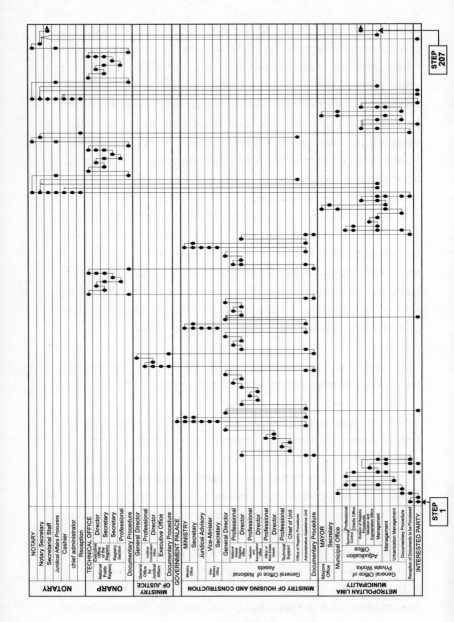

Figure 2.1
PROCEDURES TO FORMALIZE A LEGALLY OBTAINED HOME
IN PERU CONSIST OF 5 STAGES; THE FIRST ONE ALONE
INVOLVES 207 STEPS

private bus, jitney or taxi driver who wanted to obtain official recognition of his route faced twenty-six months of red tape.

My research team, with the help of local associates, has repeated similar experiments in other countries. The obstacles were no less formidable than in Peru; often they were even more daunting. In the Philippines, if a person has built a dwelling in a settlement on either state- or privately owned urban land, to purchase it legally he would have to form an association with his neighbours in order to qualify for a state housing finance programme. The entire process could necessitate 168 steps, involving 53 public and private agencies and taking 13 to 25 years (see Figure 2.2). And that assumes the state housing finance programme has sufficient funds. If the dwelling happens to be in an area still considered 'agricultural', the settler will have to clear additional hurdles for converting that land to urban use – 45 additional bureaucratic procedures before 13 entities, adding another 2 years to his quest.

In Egypt the person who wants to acquire and legally register a lot on state-owned desert land must wend his way through at least 77 bureaucratic procedures at 31 public and private agencies (see Figure 2.3). This can take anywhere from 5 to 14 years. To build a legal dwelling on former agricultural land would require 6 to 11 years of bureaucratic wrangling, maybe longer. This explains why 4.7 million Egyptians have chosen to build their dwellings illegally. If, after building his home, a settler decides he would now like to be a law-abiding citizen and purchase the rights to his dwelling, he risks having it demolished, paying a steep fine, and serving up to ten years in prison.

In Haiti one way an ordinary citizen can settle legally on government land is first to lease it from the government for five years and then buy it. Working with associates in Haiti, our researchers found that to obtain such a lease took 65 bureaucratic steps – requiring, on average, a little more than 2

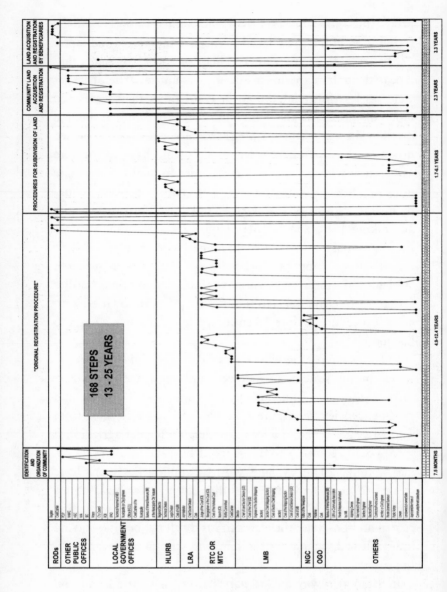

Figure 2.2
PROCEDURES TO FORMALIZE INFORMAL URBAN PROPERTY
IN THE PHILIPPINES

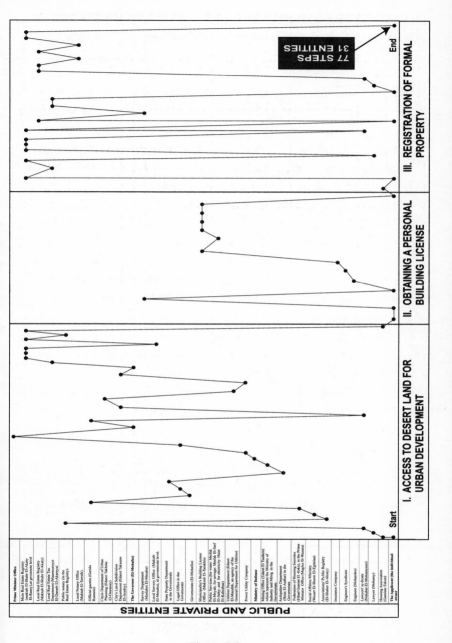

Figure 2.3

PROCEDURES TO GAIN ACCESS TO DESERT LAND FOR BUILDING PURPOSES AND TO REGISTER THESE PROPERTY RIGHTS IN EGYPT (6-14 YEARS)

years – all for the privilege of merely leasing the land for 5 years. To buy the land required another 111 bureaucratic hurdles, and 12 more years (see Figure 2.4). Total time to gain lawful land in Haiti: 19 years. Yet even this long ordeal will not ensure that the property remains legal.

In every country we investigated we found that it is very nearly as difficult to *stay* legal as it is to *become* legal. Inevitably, migrants do not so much break the law as the law breaks them – and they opt out of the system. In 1976 two-thirds of those who worked in Venezuela were employed in legally established enterprises; today the proportion is less than half. Thirty years ago more than two-thirds of the new housing erected in Brazil was intended for rent. Today, only about 3 per cent of new construction is officially listed as rental housing. To where did that market vanish? To the extralegal areas of Brazilian cities called *favelas*, which operate outside the highly regulated formal economy and function according to supply and demand. There are no rent controls in the *favelas*; rents are paid in US dollars and renters who do not pay are rapidly evacuated.

Once these newcomers to the city quit the system, they become 'extralegal'. Their only alternative is to live and work outside the official law, using their own informally binding arrangements to protect and mobilize their assets. These arrangements result from a combination of rules selectively borrowed from the official legal system, *ad hoc* improvisations and customs brought from their places of origin or locally devised. They are held together by a social contract that is upheld by a community as a whole and enforced by authorities the community has selected. These extralegal social contracts have created a vibrant but undercapitalized sector, the centre of the world of the poor.

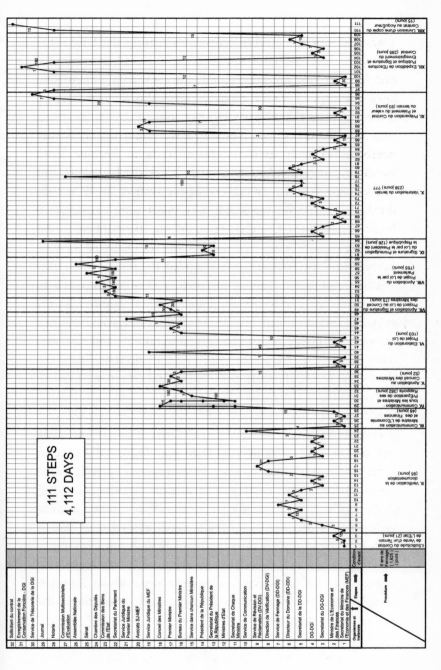

Figure 2.4
PROCEDURES TO OBTAIN A SALES (VENTE) CONTRACT
FOLLOWING THE 5 YEAR LEASE CONTRACT IN HAITI

The Undercapitalized Sector

Although the migrants are refugees from the law, they have hardly retreated into idleness. Undercapitalized sectors throughout the Third World and ex-communist countries buzz with hard work and ingenuity. Street-side cottage industries have sprung up everywhere, manufacturing anything from clothing and footwear to imitation Cartier watches and Vuitton bags. There are workshops that build and rebuild machinery, cars, even buses. The new urban poor have created entire industries and neighbourhoods that have to operate on clandestine connections to electricity and water. There are even dentists who fill cavities without a licence.

This is not just a story of the poor serving the poor. These new entrepreneurs are filling the gaps in the legal economy as well. Unauthorized buses, jitneys and taxis account for most of the public transportation in many developing countries. In other parts of the Third World, vendors from the shanty towns supply most of the food available in the market, whether from carts on the street or from stalls in buildings they construct.

In 1993 the Mexican Chamber of Commerce estimated the number of street-vendor stands in the Federal District of Mexico City at 150,000, with an additional 293,000 in 43 other Mexican centres. These tiny booths average just 1.5 metres wide. If the Mexico City vendors lined up their stands on a single street with no gaps at intersections, they would form a continuous row more than 210 kilometres long. Thousands upon thousands of people work in the extralegal sector – on the streets, from their homes and in the city's unregistered shops, offices and factories. An attempt by the Mexican National Statistics Institute in 1994 to measure the number of informal 'microbusinesses' in the entire country came up with a total of 2.65 million.

These are all real-life examples of economic life in the undercapitalized sector of society. In the former communist nations you may see even more sophisticated activities off the books, from the production of computer hardware and software to the manufacture of jet fighters for sale abroad.

Russia, of course, has quite a different history from Third World countries such as Haiti and the Philippines. Nevertheless, since the fall of communism, the former Soviet states have been slipping into the same patterns of informal ownership. In 1995 *Business Week* reported that four years after the end of communism, only 'some 280,000 farmers out of 10 million own their land' in Russia. Another report paints a familiar Third World picture: '[In the former Soviet Union] rights of private possession, use, and alienation of land are inadequately defined and not clearly protected by law . . . Mechanisms used in market economies to protect land rights are still in their infancy . . . The State itself continues to restrict use rights on land that it does not own.'[3] Estimates based on electricity consumption indicate that between 1989 and 1994 unofficial activity in former Soviet states increased from 12 per cent to 37 per cent of total production. Some put the proportion even higher.

None of this will come as news to those who live outside the West. You need only open a window or take a taxi from the airport to your hotel to see city perimeters crowded with homes, armies of vendors hawking wares in the streets, glimpses of bustling workshops behind garage doors and battered busses crisscrossing the grimy streets. Extralegality is often perceived as a 'marginal' issue similar to black markets in advanced nations, or poverty, or unemployment. The extralegal world is typically viewed as a place where gangsters roam, sinister characters of interest only to the police, anthropologists and missionaries.

In fact it is legality that is marginal; extralegality has become the norm. The poor have already taken control of vast quantities of real estate and production. Those international agencies that jet their consultants to the gleaming glass towers of the elegant quadrants of town to meet with the local 'private sector' are talking to only a fraction of the entrepreneurial world. The emerging economic powers of the Third World and former communist nations are the garbage collectors, the appliance manufacturers and the illegal construction companies in the streets far below. The only real choice for the governments of these nations is whether they are going to integrate those resources into an orderly and coherent legal framework or continue to live in anarchy.

How Much Dead Capital?

Over the past decade my researchers, assisted by knowledgeable local professionals, have made surveys of five Third World cities – Cairo, Lima, Manila, Mexico City and Port-au-Prince – in an effort to gauge the value of the possessions of those people who have been locked out of the capitalized economy by discriminatory laws. (These results are graphically summarized in the charts in the Appendix.) To be more confident of our results, we focused our attention on the most tangible and detectable of assets: real estate.

Unlike the sale of food or shoes, auto repair, or the manufacture of phoney Cartier watches – activities that are difficult to count and even more difficult to value – buildings cannot be hidden. You can ascertain their value simply by surveying the cost of the building materials and observing the selling prices of comparable buildings. We spent many thousands of days counting buildings block by block. Wherever authorized to do so, we published our results obtained in each country, so that they could be openly discussed and criticized. In collaboration with people on the spot we tested and retested our methods and results.

We discovered that the way the people build in the under-capitalized sector takes as many forms as there are legal obstacles to circumvent. The most obvious examples are the shanties built on government-owned land. But our researchers discovered far more creative ways of getting around the real estate laws. In Peru, for instance, people formed agricultural cooperatives to buy estates from their old owners and to convert them into housing and industrial settlements. Because there are no easy legal ways to change land tenure, farmers in state-owned cooperatives illegally subdivided the land into smaller, privately held parcels. As a result, few if any have valid title to their ground. In Port-au-Prince even quite expensive properties change hands without anybody bothering to inform the registry office, which is hopelessly backlogged anyway. In Manila housing springs up on land zoned solely for industrial use. In Cairo residents of older four-storey public housing projects build three illegal storeys on top of their buildings and sell the apartments to relatives and other clients. Also in Cairo the legal tenants of apartments whose rents were frozen in the early 1950s at sums now worth less than a dollar a year subdivide these properties into smaller apartments and lease them out at market prices.

Some of this housing was extralegal from day one, constructed in violation of all kinds of laws. Other buildings – the Port-au-Prince houses, the Cairo rent-controlled apart-ments – originated in the legal system but then dropped out as complying with the law became too costly and complicated. By one route or another, almost every dwelling place in the cities we surveyed exited both the legal framework and the very laws that could have hypothetically provided owners with the representations and institutions to create capital. There still may be deeds or some kind of record in someone's hands, but the real ownership status of these assets has slipped out of the official registry system, leaving records and maps outdated. The result is that most people's resources are commercially and financially invisible. Nobody really knows who owns what and where, who is accountable for the performance of obligations, who is responsible for losses and fraud, and what mechanisms are available to enforce payment for services and goods delivered. Consequently, most potential assets in these countries have not been identified or realized; there is little accessible capital, and the exchange economy is constrained and sluggish.

This picture of the undercapitalized sector is strikingly different from the conventional wisdom of the developing world. But this is where most people live. It is a world where ownership of assets is difficult to trace and validate and is governed by no legally recognizable set of rules; where the assets' potentially useful economic attributes have not been described or organized; where they cannot be used to obtain surplus value through multiple transactions because their unfixed nature and uncertainty leave too much room for misunderstanding, faulty recollection and reversal of agreement. Where most assets, in short, are dead capital.

How Much is This Dead Capital Worth?

Dead capital, virtual mountains of it, lines the streets of every developing and ex-communist country. In the Philippines, by our calculation, 57 per cent of city-dwellers and 67 per cent of people in the countryside live in housing that is dead capital. In Peru 53 per cent of city-dwellers and 81 per cent of people in the countryside live in extralegal dwellings.

The figures are even more dramatic in Haiti and Egypt. In Haiti, also according to our surveys, 68 per cent of city-dwellers and 97 per cent of people in the countryside live in housing to which nobody has clear legal title. In Egypt dead-capital housing is home for 92 per cent of city-dwellers and 83 per cent of people in the countryside.

Many of these dwellings are not worth much by Western standards. A shanty in Port-au-Prince may fetch as little as $500, a cabin by a polluted waterway in Manila only $2,700, a fairly substantial house in a village outside Cairo only about $5,000, and in the hills around Lima a respectable bungalow with garage and picture-window is valued at only

$20,000. But there are a great many such dwellings, and collectively their value dramatically outweighs the total wealth of the rich.

In Haiti untitled rural and urban real estate holdings are together worth some $5.2 billion. To put that in context, this sum is four times the total of all the assets of all the legally operating companies in Haiti, nine times the value of all assets owned by the government and 158 times the value of all foreign direct investment in Haiti's recorded history to 1995. Is Haiti an exception, a part of Francophone Africa mistakenly put into the American hemisphere, where the Duvalier regime delayed the emergence of a systematized legal system? Perhaps.

Then let's consider Peru, a Hispanic–Indo-American country with a very different tradition and ethnic make-up. The value of extralegally held rural and urban real estate in Peru amounts to some $74 billion. This is five times the total valuation of the Lima Stock Exchange before the slump of 1998, eleven times greater than the value of potentially privatizable government enterprises and facilities, and fourteen times the value of all foreign direct investment in the country through its documented history. Would you counter that Peru's formal economy has also been stunted by the trad-itions of the ancient Inca Empire, the corrupting influence of colonial Spain and the recent war with the Maoist Sendero Luminoso?

Very well, then consider the Philippines, a former Asian pro-tectorate of the United States. The value of untitled real estate there is $133 billion, four times the capitalization of the 216 domestic companies listed on the Philippines Stock Exchange, seven times the total deposits in the country's commercial banks, nine times the total capital of state-owned enterprises, and fourteen times the value of all foreign direct investment.

Perhaps the Philippines, too, is an anomaly – something to do with how Christianity developed in former Spanish colonies. If so, let's consider Egypt. The value of Egypt's dead capital in real estate is, by the tally we made with our Egyptian colleagues, some $240 billion. That is thirty times the value of all the shares on the Cairo Stock Exchange and, as I mentioned, fifty-five times the value of all foreign investment in Egypt.

In every country we have examined, the entrepreneurial ingenuity of the poor has created wealth on a vast scale – wealth that also constitutes by far the largest source of potential capital for development. These assets not only far exceed the holdings of the government, the local stock exchanges and foreign direct investment; they are many times greater than all the aid from advanced nations and all the loans extended by the World Bank.

The results are even more astonishing when we take the data from the four countries we have studied and project it over the Third World and former communist nations as a whole. We estimate that about 85 per cent of urban parcels in these nations, and between 40 per cent and 53 per cent of rural parcels, are held in such a way that they cannot be used to create capital. Putting a value on all these assets is inevitably going to come up with a rough number. But we believe that our estimates are as accurate as they can be and quite conservative.

By our calculations, the total value of the real estate held but not legally owned by the poor of the Third World and former communist nations is at least $9.3 trillion (see Table 2.1).

This is a number worth pondering: $9.3 trillion is about twice as much as the total circulating US money supply. It is very nearly as much as the total value of all the companies listed on the main stock exchanges of the world's twenty most developed countries: New York, Tokyo, London, Frankfurt, Toronto, Paris, Milan, the NASDAQ and a dozen others. It is more than twenty times the total direct foreign investment into all Third World and former communist countries in the ten years after 1989, forty-six times as much as all the World Bank loans of the past three decades, and ninety-

URBAN

	Total Population (millions)	Urban Population (%)	Urban Population (millions)	Urban Dwellings (millions)	Informal Urban Dwellings[2] (millions)	Value of Informal Urban Dwellings (trillion US$)
ASIA	1,747	29%	503	101	85	1.75
AFRICA	525	32%	167	33	28	0.58
MIDDLE EAST & NORTH AFRICA	371	57%	211	42	36	0.74
SOUTH AMERICA	328	78%	256	51	44	0.89
MEXICO, CENTRAL AMERICA AND THE CARRIBEAN	161	64%	103	21	18	0.36
China, NIS and Eastern Europe	1,611	38%	619	124	105	2.16
SUBTOTAL	**4,743**		**1,859**	**372**	**316**	**6.48**
Other Developing Countries	191	39%	75	15	13	0.26
TOTAL	**4,934**		**1,934**	**387**	**329**	**6.74**

RURAL

	Rural Area (thousand ha)	Informality in Rural Areas (%)	Informal Rural Area (thousand ha)	Informal Rural Area: Croplands (thousand ha)	Informal Rural Area: Grasslands (thousand ha)	Value of informal Rural Area[3] (trillion US$)
ASIA	489,586	44%	215,164	147,798	67,365	0.59
AFRICA	738,639	50%	368,792	88,166	280,626	0.39
MIDDLE EAST & NORTH AFRICA	444,665	40%	177,866	59,660	118,206	0.25
SOUTH AMERICA	607,407	49%	297,895	51,006	246,889	0.24
MEXICO, CENTRAL AMERICA AND THE CARRIBEAN	134,541	53%	71,025	20,813	50,212	0.09
China, NIS and Eastern Europe	1,151,280	47%	540,142	188,721	351,421	0.80
SUBTOTAL	**3,566,118**		**1,670,884**	**556,164**	**1,114,719**	**2.36**
Other Developing Countries	359,926	47%	169,165	56,308	112,857	0.24
TOTAL	**3,926,044**		**1,840,049**	**612,472**	**1,227,576**	**2.60**

TOTAL INFORMAL   US $ 9.34 trillion

1/ 179 developing and former communist nations.
2/ It is estimated that 85% of urban parcels is informal. They either: i) were built in violation of express laws; ii) did not comply with requirements for access to land; iii) were originally formal but became informal; or iv) were built by the government without complying with legal requirements.
3/ A value of US$ 3,973 per hectare of croplands and of US$ 138 per hectare of grasslands were used.

Table 2.1
URBAN AND RURAL DEAD CAPITAL IN REAL ESTATE
WORLDWIDE [1] (1997)

three times as much as all development assistance from all advanced countries to the Third World in the same period.

Acres of Diamonds

The words 'international poverty' too easily bring to mind images of destitute beggars sleeping on the kerbsides of Calcutta and hungry African children starving on the sand. These scenes are, of course, real, and millions of our fellow human beings demand and deserve our help. Nevertheless, the grimmest picture of the Third World is not the most accurate. Worse, it draws attention away from the arduous achievements of those small entrepreneurs who have triumphed over every imaginable obstacle to create the greater part of the wealth of their society. A truer image would depict a man and woman who have painstakingly saved to construct a house for themselves and their children, and who are creating enterprises where nobody imagined they could be built. I resent the characterization of such heroic entrepreneurs as contributors to the problem of global poverty.

They are not the problem. They are the solution.

In the years after the American Civil War a lecturer named Russell Conwell crisscrossed America delivering a message that stirred millions of people. He told the story of an Indian merchant who had been promised by a prophet that he would surely become rich beyond all imagining if only he would seek his treasure. The merchant travelled the world only to return home old, sad and defeated. As he re-entered his abandoned house, he needed a drink of water. But the well on his property had silted up. Wearily, he took out his spade and dug a new one – and instantly struck the Golconda, the world's greatest diamond mine.

Conwell's message is a useful one. Leaders of the Third World and former communist nations need not wander the world's foreign ministries and international financial institutions seeking their fortune. In the midst of their own poorest neighbourhoods and shanty towns there are – if not acres of diamonds – trillions of dollars, all ready to be put to use if only we can unravel the mystery of how assets are transformed into live capital.

3

THE MYSTERY OF CAPITAL

*The sense of the world must lie outside the world. In the world
everything is as it is and happens as it does happen. In it there is
no value – and if there were, it would be of no value.*

*If there is a value which is of value, it must lie outside all
happening and being-so. For all happening and being-so is
accidental.*

*What makes it non-accidental cannot lie in the world, for
otherwise this would again be accidental.*

It must lie outside the world.

LUDWIG WITTGENSTEIN, *Tractatus Logico-Philosophicus*

Walk down most roads in the Middle East, the former Soviet
Union or Latin America, and you will see several things:
houses used for shelter, parcels of land being tilled, sowed
and harvested, merchandise being bought and sold. Assets in
developing and former communist countries primarily serve
these immediate physical purposes. In the West, however, the
same assets also lead a parallel life as capital outside the
physical world. They can be used to put in motion more production by securing the interests of other parties as 'collateral'
for a mortgage, for example, or by assuring the supply of other
forms of credit and public utilities.

Why can't buildings and land elsewhere in the world also lead this parallel life? Why can't the enormous resources we discussed in Chapter 2 – $9.3 trillion of dead capital – produce value beyond their 'natural' state? My reply is: Dead capital exists because we have forgotten (or perhaps never realized) that converting a physical asset to generate capital – using your house to borrow money to finance an enterprise, for example – requires a very complex process. It is similar to the process that Einstein taught us whereby a single brick can be made to release a huge amount of energy in the form of an atomic explosion. By analogy, capital is the result of discovering and unleashing potential energy from the trillions of bricks that the poor have accumulated in their buildings.

There is, however, one crucial difference between unleashing energy from a brick and unleashing capital from brick buildings: while humanity (or at least a large group of scientists) has mastered the process of obtaining energy from matter, we seem to have forgotten the process that allows us to obtain capital from assets. The result is that 80 per cent of the world is undercapitalized; people cannot draw economic life from their buildings (or any other asset) to generate capital. Worse, the advanced nations seem unable to teach them. Why assets can be made to produce abundant capital in the West but very little in the rest of the world is a mystery.

Clues from the Past (from Smith to Marx)

To unravel the mystery of capital, we have to go back to the seminal meaning of the word. In medieval Latin 'capital' appears to have denoted head of cattle or other livestock, which have always been important sources of wealth beyond the basic meat they provide. Livestock are low-maintenance possessions; they are mobile and can be moved away from danger; they are also easy to count and measure. But most important, from livestock you can obtain additional wealth, or surplus value, by setting in motion other industries, including milk, hides, wool, meat and fuel. Livestock also have the useful attribute of being able to reproduce themselves. Thus the term 'capital' begins to do two jobs simultaneously, capturing the physical dimension of assets (livestock) as well as their potential to generate surplus value. From the barnyard, it was only a short step to the desks of the inventors of economics, who generally defined 'capital' as that part of a country's assets that initiates surplus production and increases productivity.

Great classical economists such as Adam Smith and Karl Marx believed that capital was the engine that powered the market economy. Capital was considered to be the principal part of the economic whole – the pre-eminent factor as in such phrases as *capital* issues, *capital* punishment, the *capital* city of a country. They wanted to understand what capital is and how it is produced and accumulated. Whether you agree with the classical economists or not, or perhaps view them as irrelevant (maybe Smith never understood that the Industrial Revolution was under way, maybe Marx's labour theory of value has no practical application), there is no doubt that these thinkers built the towering edifices of thought on which we can now stand and try to find out what capital is, what produces it and why non-Western nations generate so little of it.

For Smith, economic specialization – the division of labour and the subsequent exchange of products in the market – was the source of increasing productivity and therefore 'the wealth of nations'. What made this specialization and exchange possible was capital, which Smith defined as the stock of assets accumulated for productive purposes. Entrepreneurs could use their accumulated resources to support specialized enterprises until they could exchange their products for the other things they needed. The more capital was accumulated, the more specialization became possible, and the higher society's productivity would be. Marx agreed; for him, the wealth capitalism produces presents itself as an immense pile of commodities.

Smith believed that the phenomenon of capital was a consequence of man's natural progression from a hunting, rural and agricultural society to a commercial one where, through interdependence, specialization and trade, he could increase his productive powers immensely. Capital was to be the magic that would enhance productivity and create surplus value. 'The quantity of industry', wrote Smith, 'not only increases in every country with the increase of the stock [capital] which employs it, but, in consequence of that increase, the same quantity of industry produces a much greater quantity of work.'[1]

Smith emphasized one point that is at the very heart of the mystery we are trying to solve: for accumulated assets to become active capital and put additional production in motion, they must be *fixed and realized in some particular subject* 'which lasts for some time at least after that labour is past. It is, as it were, a certain quantity of labour stocked and stored up to be employed, if necessary, upon some other occasion.'[2] Smith warned that labour invested in the production of assets would not leave any trace or value if not properly *fixed*.

What Smith really meant may be the subject of legitimate debate. What I take from him, however, is that capital is not the accumulated stock of assets but the *potential* it holds to deploy new production. This potential is, of course, abstract. It must be processed and fixed into a tangible form before we can release it – just like the potential nuclear energy in Einstein's brick. Without a conversion process – one that draws out and fixes the potential energy contained in the brick – there is no explosion; a brick is just a brick. Creating capital also requires a conversion process.

This notion – that capital is first an abstract concept and must be given a fixed, tangible form to be useful – was familiar to other classical economists. Simonde de Sismondi, the nineteenth-century Swiss economist, wrote that capital was 'a permanent value, that multiplies and does not perish . . . Now this value detaches itself from the product that creates it, it becomes a metaphysical and insubstantial quantity always in the possession of whoever produced it, for whom this value could [be fixed in] different forms.'[3] The great French economist Jean Baptiste Say believed that 'capital is always immaterial by nature since it is not matter which makes capital but the value of that matter, value has nothing corporeal about it'[4]. Marx agreed; for him, a table could be made of something material, like wood, 'but so soon as it steps forth as a commodity, it is changed into something transcendent. It not only stands with its feet on the ground, but, in relation to all other commodities, it stands on its head, and evolves out of its wooden brain grotesque ideas, far more wonderful than table-turning ever was.'[5]

This essential meaning of capital has been lost to history. Capital is now confused with money, which is only one of the many forms in which it travels. It is always easier to remember a difficult concept in one of its tangible manifestations than in its essence. The mind wraps itself around 'money' more easily than 'capital'. But it is a mistake to assume that money is what finally fixes capital. As Adam Smith pointed out, money is the 'great wheel of circulation', but it is *not* capital because value 'cannot consist in those metal pieces'.[6] In other words, money facilitates transactions, allowing us to buy and sell things, but it is not itself the progenitor of additional production. As Smith insisted, 'the gold and silver money, which circulates in any country, may very properly be compared to a highway, which, while it circulates and carries to market all the grass and corn of the country, produces itself not a single pile of either'.[7]

Much of the mystery of capital dissipates as soon as you stop thinking of 'capital' as a synonym for 'money saved and invested'. The misapprehension that it is money that fixes capital comes about, I suspect, because modern business expresses the value of capital in terms of money. It is hard to estimate the total value of a collection of assets of very different types, such as machinery, buildings and land, without resorting to money. After all, that is why money was invented; it provides a standard index to measure the value of things so that we may exchange dissimilar assets. But as useful as it is, money cannot fix in any way the abstract potential of a particular asset in order to convert it into capital. Third World and former communist nations are infamous for inflating their economies with money while not being able to generate much capital.

The Potential Energy in Assets

What is it that fixes the potential of an asset so that it can put additional production into motion? What detaches value from a simple house and fixes it in a way that allows us to realize it as capital?

We can begin to find an answer by using our energy analogy. Consider a mountain lake. We can think about this lake in its immediate physical context and see some primary uses for it, such as canoeing and fishing. But when we think about this same lake as an engineer would by focusing on its capacity to generate energy as an additional value beyond the lake's natural state as a body of water, we suddenly see the potential created by the lake's elevated position. The challenge for the engineer is finding out how he can create a *process* that allows him to convert and fix this potential into a form that can be used to do additional work. In the case of the elevated lake that process is contained in a hydroelectric plant that allows the lake water to move rapidly downward with the force of gravity, thereby transforming the placid lake's energy potential into the kinetic energy of tumbling water. This new kinetic energy may then rotate turbines, creating mechanical energy that may be used to turn electromagnets that further convert it into electrical energy. As electricity, the potential energy of the placid lake is now fixed in the form necessary to produce controllable current that may be further transmitted through wire conductors to faraway places to deploy new production.

Thus an apparently placid lake may be used to illuminate your room and power the machinery in a factory. What was required was an external man-made process, which allowed us, first, to identify the potential of the weight of the water to do additional work; and, second, to convert this potential energy into electricity that may be used to create surplus value. The additional value we obtain from the lake is not a value of the lake itself (like a precious ore intrinsic to the earth), but rather a value of the man-made process *extrinsic* to the lake. It is this process that allows us to transform the lake from a fishing and canoeing kind of place into an energy-producing kind of place.

Capital, like energy, is also a dormant value. Bringing it to life requires us to go beyond *looking* at our assets as they are to *thinking* actively about them as they could be. It requires a process for fixing an asset's economic potential into a form that may be used to initiate additional production.

Yet, while the process that converts the potential energy in the water into electricity is well known, the one that gives assets the form required to put in motion more production is not known. In other words, while we know that it is the penstock, turbines, generators, transformers and wires of the hydroelectric energy system that convert the potential energy of the lake until it is fixed in an accessible form, we do not know where to find the key process that converts the economic potential of a house into capital.

This is because that key process was not deliberately set up to create capital, but for the more mundane purpose of protecting property ownership. As the property systems of Western nations grew, they developed, imperceptibly, a variety of mechanisms that gradually combined into a process that churned out capital as never before. Although we use these mechanisms all the time, we do not realize that they have capital-generating functions because they do not wear that label. We view them as parts of the system that protects property, not as interlocking mechanisms for fixing the economic potential of an asset in such a way that it can be converted into capital. What creates capital in the West, in other words, is an implicit process buried in the intricacies of its formal property systems.

The Hidden Conversion Process of the West

This may sound too simple or too complex. But consider whether it is possible for assets to be used productively if they do not belong to something or someone. Where do we confirm the existence of these assets and the transactions that transform them and raise their productivity if not in the context of a formal property system? Where do we record the relevant economic features of assets if not in the records and titles that formal property systems provide? Where are the codes of conduct that govern the use and transfer of assets if not in the framework of formal property systems? It is formal property that provides the process, the forms and the rules that fix assets in a condition that allows us to realize them as active capital.

In the West this formal property system begins to process assets into capital by describing and organizing the most economically and socially useful aspects *about* assets, preserving this information in a recording system – as insertions in a written ledger or a blip on a computer disk – and then embodying them in a title. A set of detailed and precise legal rules governs this entire process. Formal property records and titles thus represent our shared concept of what is economically meaningful about any asset. They capture and organize all the relevant information required to conceptualize the potential value of an asset and so allow us to control it. Property is the realm where we identify and explore assets, combine them and link them to other assets. The formal property system is capital's hydroelectric plant. This is the place where capital is born.

Any asset whose economic and social aspects are not fixed in a formal property system is extremely hard to move in the market. How can the huge amounts of assets changing hands in a modern market economy be controlled if not through a formal property process? Without such a system, any trade of an asset, say a piece of real estate, requires an enormous effort just to determine the basics of the transaction: does the seller own the real estate and have the right to transfer it? Can he pledge it? Will the new owner be accepted as such by those who enforce property rights? What are the effective means to exclude other claimants? In developing and former communist nations such questions are difficult to answer. For most goods, there is no place where the answers are reliably fixed. That is why the sale or lease of a house may involve lengthy and cumbersome procedures of approval involving all the neighbours. This is often the only way to verify that the owner truly owns the house and there are no other claims on it. It is also why the exchange of most assets outside the West is restricted to local circles of trading partners.

As we saw in the previous chapter, these countries' principal problem is not the lack of entrepreneurship: the poor have accumulated trillions of dollars of real estate during the last forty years. What the poor lack is easy access to the property mechanisms that could legally fix the economic potential of their assets so that they could be used to produce, secure or guarantee greater value in the expanded market. In the West every asset – every piece of land, every house, every chattel – is formally fixed in updated records governed by rules contained in the property system. Every increment in production, every new building, product or commercially valuable thing is someone's formal property. Even if assets belong to a corporation, real people still own them indirectly, through titles certifying that they own the corporation as 'shareholders'.

Like electric power, capital will not be generated if the single key facility that produces and fixes it is not in place. Just as a lake needs a hydroelectric plant to produce usable energy, assets need a formal property system to produce significant surplus value. Without formal property to extract their economic potential and convert it into a form that can be easily transported and controlled, the assets of developing and former communist countries are like water in a lake high in the Andes – an untapped stock of potential energy.

Why has the genesis of capital become such a mystery? Why have the rich nations of the world, so quick with their economic advice, not explained how indispensable formal property is to capital formation? The answer is that the process within the formal property system that breaks down assets into capital is extremely difficult to visualize. It is hidden in thousands of pieces of legislation, statutes, regulations and institutions that govern the system. Anyone trapped in such a legal morass would be hard pressed to figure out how the process works. The only way to see it is from outside the system – from the extralegal sector – which is where my colleagues and I do most of our work.

For some time now I have been looking at the law from an extralegal point of view, to understand better how it functions and what effects it produces. This is not as crazy as it seems. As the French philosopher Michel Foucault has argued, it may be easier to discover what something means by looking at it from the opposite side of the bridge. 'To find out what our society means by sanity', Foucault has written, 'perhaps we should investigate what is happening in the field of insanity. And what we mean by legality in the field of illegality.'[8] Moreover, property, like energy, is a concept; it cannot be experienced directly. Pure energy has never been seen or touched. And no one can see property. One can only experience energy and property by their effects.

From my viewpoint in the extralegal sector, I have seen that the formal property systems of the West produce six effects that allow their citizens to generate capital. The incapacity elsewhere in the world to deploy capital stems from the fact that most of the people in Third World and former communist countries are cut off from these essential effects.

Property Effect No. 1: Fixing the Economic Potential of Assets

The potential value locked up in a house can be revealed and transformed into active capital in the same way that potential energy is identified in a mountain lake and then transformed into actual energy. In both cases the transition from one state to another requires a process that transposes the physical object into a man-made representative universe where we can disengage the resource from its burdensome material constraints and concentrate on its potential.

Capital is born by representing in writing – in a title, a security, a contract and other such records – the most economically and socially useful qualities *about* the asset, as opposed to the visually more striking aspects *of* the asset. This is where potential value is first described and registered. The moment you focus your attention on the title of a house, for example, and not on the house itself, you have automatically stepped from the material world into the conceptual universe where capital lives. You are reading a representation that focuses your attention on the economic potential of the house by filtering out all the confusing lights and shadows of its physical aspects and its local surroundings. Formal property forces you to think about the house as an economic and social concept. It invites you to go beyond viewing the house as mere shelter – and thus a dead asset – and to see it as live capital.

The proof that property is pure concept comes when a house changes hands; nothing physically changes. Looking at a house will not tell you who owns it. A house that is yours today looks exactly as it did yesterday when it was mine. It looks the same whether I own it, rent it or sell it to you. Property is not the house itself but an economic concept *about* the house, embodied in a legal representation. This means that a formal property representation is something separate from the asset itself.

What do formal property representations have that allows them to do additional work? Are they not just simple stand-ins for the assets? No. I repeat: a formal property representation such as a title is not a reproduction *of* the house, like a photograph, but a representation of our concepts *about* the house. Specifically, it represents the non-visible qualities that have potential for producing value. These are not physical qualities of the house itself but rather economically and socially meaningful qualities we humans have attributed to the house (such as the ability to use it for a variety of purposes that may be secured by liens, mortgages, easements and other covenants).

In advanced nations this formal property representation functions as the means to secure the interests of other parties, and to create accountability by providing all the information, references, rules and enforcement mechanisms required to do so. In the West, for example, most formal property can be easily used as collateral for a loan; as equity exchanged for investment; as an address for collecting debts, rates and taxes; as a locus point for the identification of individuals for commercial, judicial or civic purposes; or as a liable terminal for receiving public utility services, such as energy, water, sewage, telephone or TV. While houses in advanced nations are acting as shelters or workplaces, their representations are leading a parallel life, carrying out a variety of additional functions to secure the interests of other parties.

Legal property thus gave the West the tools to produce surplus value over and above its physical assets. Property representations enabled people to think about assets not only through physical acquaintance but through the description of their latent economic and social qualities. Whether anyone intended it or not, the legal property system became the staircase that took these nations from the universe of assets in their natural state to the conceptual universe of capital, where assets can be viewed in their full productive potential.

With legal property, the advanced nations of the West had the key to modern development; their citizens now had the means to discover, with great facility and on an ongoing basis, the most potentially productive qualities of their resources. As Aristotle discovered 2,300 years ago, what you can do with things increases infinitely when you focus your thinking on their potential. By learning to fix the economic potential of their assets through property records, Westerners created a fast track to explore the most productive aspects of their possessions. Formal property became the staircase to the conceptual realm where the economic meaning of things can be discovered and where capital is born.

Property Effect No. 2: Integrating Dispersed Information into One System

As we saw in the previous chapter, most people in developing and former communist nations cannot enter the legal property system, such as it is, no matter how hard they try. Because they cannot insert their assets into the legal property system, they end up holding them extralegally. The reason capitalism has triumphed in the West and faltered in the rest of the world is because most of the assets in Western nations have been integrated into one formal representational system.

This integration did not happen casually. Over decades in the nineteenth century, politicians, legislators and judges pulled together the scattered facts and rules that had governed property throughout cities, villages, buildings and farms and integrated them into one system. This 'pulling together' of property representations, a revolutionary moment in the history of developed nations, deposited all the information and rules governing the accumulated wealth of their citizens into one knowledge base. Before that moment, information about assets was far less accessible. Every farm or settlement recorded its assets and the rules governing them in rudimentary ledgers, symbols or oral testimony. But the information was atomized, dispersed and not available to any one agent at any given moment. As we know too well today, an abundance of facts is not necessarily an abundance of knowledge. For knowledge to be functional, advanced nations had to integrate into one comprehensive system all their loose and isolated data about property.

Developing and former communist nations have not done this. In all the countries I have studied I have never found just one legal system but dozens or even hundreds, managed by all sorts of organizations, some legal, others extralegal, ranging from small entrepreneurial groups to housing organizations. Consequently, what people in those countries can do with their property is limited to the imagination of the owners and their acquaintances. In Western countries, where property information is standardized and universally available, what owners can do with their assets benefits from the collective imagination of a larger network of people.

It may surprise the Western reader that most of the world's nations have yet to integrate extralegal property agreements into one formal legal system. For Westerners, there supposedly is only one law – the official one. Yet the West's reliance on integrated property systems is a phenomenon at most of the last two hundred years. In most Western countries integrated property systems appeared only about a hundred years ago; Japan's integration happened little more than fifty years ago. As we shall see in detail later, diverse informal property arrangements were once the norm in every nation. Legal pluralism was the standard in continental Europe until Roman law was rediscovered in the fourteenth century and governments assembled all currents of law into one coordinated system.

In California just after the gold rush of 1849 there were some eight hundred separate property jurisdictions, each with its own records and individual regulations established by local consensus. Throughout the United States, from California to Florida, claim associations agreed on their own rules and elected their own officers. It took more than one hundred years, well into the late nineteenth century, for the US government to pass special statutes that integrated and formalized US assets. By enacting more than thirty-five pre-emption and mining statutes, Congress gradually managed to integrate into one system the informal property rules created by millions of immigrants and squatters. The result was an integrated property market that fuelled the United States' explosive economic growth thereafter.

The reason why it is so hard to follow this history of the integration of widespread property systems is that the process took place over a very long time. Formal property registries began to appear in Germany, for example, in the twelfth century, but were not fully integrated until 1896, when the *Grundbuch* system for recording land transactions began operating on a national scale. In Japan the national campaign to formalize the property of farmers began in the late nineteenth century and ended only in the late 1940s. Switzerland's extraordinary efforts to bring together the disparate systems that protected property and transactions at the turn of the twentieth century are still not well known, even to many Swiss.

As a result of integration, citizens in advanced nations can obtain descriptions of the economic and social qualities of any available asset without having to see the asset itself. They no longer need to travel around the country to visit each and every owner and their neighbours; the formal property system lets them know what assets are available and what opportunities exist to create surplus value. Consequently, an asset's potential has become easier to evaluate and exchange, enhancing the production of capital.

Property Effect No. 3: Making People Accountable

The integration of all property systems under one formal

property law shifted the legitimacy of the rights of owners from the politicized context of local communities to the impersonal context of law. Releasing owners from restrictive local arrangements and bringing them into a more integrated legal system facilitated their accountability.

By transforming people with property interests into accountable individuals, formal property created individuals from masses. People no longer needed to rely on neighbourhood relationships or to make local arrangements to protect their rights to assets. Freed from primitive economic activities and burdensome parochial constraints, they could explore how to generate surplus value from their own assets. But there was a price to pay: once inside a formal property system owners lost their anonymity. By becoming inextricably linked to real estate and businesses that could be easily identified and located, people forfeited the ability to lose themselves in the masses. The anonymity option has practically disappeared in the West, while individual accountability has been reinforced. People who do not pay for goods or services they have consumed can be identified, charged interest penalties, fined, embargoed and have their credit ratings downgraded. Authorities are able to learn about legal infractions and dishonoured contracts; they can suspend services, place liens against property and withdraw some or all of the privileges of legal property.

Respect in Western nations for property and transactions is hardly encoded in their citizens' DNA; it is rather the result of having enforceable formal property systems. Formal property's role in protecting not only ownership but the security of transactions encourages citizens in advanced countries to respect titles, honour contracts and obey the law. When any citizen fails to act honourably, his breach is recorded in the system, jeopardizing his reputation as a trustworthy party to his neighbours, utilities, banks, telephone companies, insurance firms and the rest of the network to which property ties him.

Thus the formal property systems of the West have bestowed mixed blessings. While they provided hundreds of millions of citizens with a stake in the capitalist game, what made this stake meaningful was that it could be lost. A great part of the potential value of legal property is derived from the possibility of forfeiture. Consequently, a great deal of its power comes from the accountability it creates, from the constraints it imposes, the rules it spawns and the sanctions it can apply. By allowing people to see the economic and social potential of assets, formal property changed the perception in advanced societies of not only the potential rewards of using assets but the dangers of doing so. Legal property invited commitment.

The lack of legal property thus explains why citizens in developing and former communist nations cannot make profitable contracts with strangers, cannot get credit, insurance or utilities services: they have no property to lose. Because they have no property to lose, they are taken seriously as contracting parties only by their immediate family and neighbours. People with nothing to lose are trapped in the grubby basement of the pre-capitalist world.

Meanwhile, citizens of advanced nations can contract for practically anything that is reasonable, but the entry price is commitment. And commitment is better understood when backed up by a pledge of property, whether it be a mortgage, a lien or any other form of security that protects the other contracting party.

Property Effect No. 4: Making Assets Fungible

One of the most important things a formal property system does is transform assets from a less to a more accessible condition, so that they can do additional work. Unlike physical assets, representations are easily combined, divided, mobilized and used to stimulate business deals. By uncoupling the economic features of an asset from its rigid, physical state, a representation makes the asset 'fungible' – able to be fashioned to suit practically any transaction.

By describing all assets in standard categories, an integrated formal property system makes possible the comparison of two architecturally different buildings constructed for the same purpose. This allows one to discriminate quickly and inexpensively between similarities and differences in assets without having to deal with each asset as if it were unique.

Standard property descriptions in the West are also written to facilitate the combination of assets. Formal property rules require assets to be described and characterized in a way that not only outlines their singularity but points out their similarity to other assets, thus making potential combinations more obvious. Through the use of standardized records, one can determine (on the basis of zoning restrictions, who the neighbours are and what they are doing, the square footage of the buildings, whether they can be joined, etc.) how to exploit a particular piece of real estate most profitably, whether as office space, for hotel rooms, a bookshop or squash courts and a sauna.

Representations also enable the division of assets without touching them. While an asset such as a factory may be an indivisible unit in the real world, in the conceptual universe of formal property representation it can be subdivided into any number of portions. Citizens of advanced nations are thus able to split most of their assets into shares, each of which can be owned by different persons, with different rights, to carry out different functions. Thanks to formal property, a single factory can be held by countless investors, who can divest themselves of their property without affecting the integrity of the physical asset.

Similarly, in a developed country, the farmer's son who wishes to follow in his father's footsteps can keep the farm by buying out his more commercially minded siblings. Farmers in many developing countries have no such option and must continually subdivide their farms for each generation until the parcels are too small to farm profitably, leaving the descendants with two alternatives: starving or stealing.

Formal property representations can also serve as movable stand-ins for physical assets, enabling owners and entrepreneurs to simulate hypothetical situations in order to explore other profitable uses of their assets – much as military officers plan their strategy for a battle by moving symbols of their troops and weapons around a map. If you think about it, it is property representations that allow entrepreneurs to simulate business strategies to grow their companies and build capital.

In addition, all standard formal property documents are crafted in such a way as to facilitate the easy measurement of an asset's attributes. If standard descriptions of assets were not readily available, anyone who wanted to buy, rent or give credit against an asset would have to expend enormous resources comparing and evaluating it against other assets – which also would lack standard descriptions. By providing standards, Western formal property systems have significantly reduced the transaction costs of mobilizing and using assets.

Once assets are in a formal property system, they endow their owners with an enormous advantage in that they can be divided and combined in more ways than a Meccano set. Westerners may adapt their assets to any economic circumstance to produce continually higher valued mixtures, while their Third World counterparts remain trapped in the physical world of rigid, non-fungible forms.

Property Effect No. 5: Networking People

By making assets fungible – capable of being divided, combined or mobilized to suit any transaction – by attaching owners to assets, assets to addresses, and ownership to enforcement, and by making information on the history of assets and owners easily accessible, formal property systems converted the citizens of the West into a network of individually identifiable and accountable business agents. The formal property process created a whole infrastructure of connecting devices that, like a railway switchyard, allowed the assets (trains) to run safely between people (stations). Formal property's contribution to mankind is not the protection of ownership; squatters, housing organizations, mafias and even primitive tribes manage to protect their assets quite efficiently. Property's real breakthrough is that it radically improved the flow of communications about assets and their potential. It also enhanced the status of their owners, who became economic agents able to transform assets within a broader network.

This explains how legal property encourages the suppliers of such utilities as electricity and water to invest in production and distribution facilities to service buildings. By legally attaching the buildings where the services will be delivered to their owners, who will be using and paying for the services, a formal property system reduces the risk of theft of services. It also reduces the financial losses from bill-collecting among people hard to locate, as well as technical losses from incorrectly estimating the electricity needs of areas where businesses and residents are clandestine and not recorded. Without knowing who has the rights to what, and without an integrated legal system where the ability to enforce obligations has been transferred from extralegal groups to government, utilities would be hard pressed to deliver services profitably. On what other basis could they identify subscribers, create utility subscription contracts, establish service connections and ensure access to parcels and buildings? How would they implement billing systems, meter-reading, collection mechanisms, loss control, fraud control, delinquent charging procedures and enforcement services such as meter shut-offs?

Buildings are always the terminals of public utilities. What transforms them into *accountable* and *responsible* terminals is legal property. Anyone who doubts this need only look at the utility situation outside the West, where technical and financial losses plus theft of services account for 30 to 50 per cent of all available utilities.

Western legal property also provides businesses with information about assets and their owners, verifiable addresses and objective records of property value, all of which lead to credit records. This information and the existence of integrated law make risk more manageable by spreading it through insurance-type devices, as well as by pooling property to secure debts.

Few seem to have noticed that the legal property system of an advanced nation is the centre of a complex web of connections that equips ordinary citizens to form ties with both the government and the private sector, and so to obtain additional goods and services. Without the tools of formal property, it is hard to see how assets could be used for everything they accomplish in the West. How else could financial organizations identify trustworthy potential borrowers on a massive scale? How could physical objects, like timber in Oregon, secure an industrial investment in Chicago? How could insurance companies find and contract customers who will pay their bills? How could information brokerage or inspection and verification services be provided efficiently and cheaply? How could tax collection work?

It is the property system that draws out the abstract potential from buildings and fixes it in representations that allow us to go beyond passively using the buildings only as shelters. Many title systems in developing nations fail to produce capital because they do not acknowledge that property can go way beyond ownership. These systems function purely as an ownership inventory of deeds and maps standing in for assets, without allowing for the additional mechanisms required to create a network where assets can lead a parallel life as capital. Formal property should not be confused with such massive inventory systems as the English Domesday Book of nine hundred years ago or a luggage check operation in an international airport. Properly understood and designed, a property system creates a network through which people can assemble their assets into more valuable combinations.

Property Effect No. 6: Protecting Transactions

One important reason why the Western formal property system works like a network is that all the property records (titles, deeds, securities and contracts that describe the economically significant aspects of assets) are continually tracked and protected as they travel through time and space. Their first stop is the public agencies that are the stewards of an advanced nation's representations. Public record-keepers administer the files that contain all the economically useful descriptions of assets, whether land, buildings, chattels, ships, industries, mines or aeroplanes. These files will alert anyone eager to use an asset about things that may restrict or enhance its realization, such as encumbrances, easements, leases, arrears, bankruptcies and mortgages. The agencies also ensure that assets are adequately and accurately represented in appropriate formats that can be updated and easily accessed.

In addition to public record-keeping systems many other private services have evolved to assist parties in fixing, moving and tracking representations so that they can easily and securely produce surplus value. These include private entities that record transactions, escrow and closings organizations, abstractors, appraisers, title and fidelity insurance firms, mortgage brokers, trust services and private custodians of documents. In the United States title insurance companies further help the mobilization of representations by issuing policies to cover parties for specified risks, ranging from defects on titles to unenforceability on mortgages and unmarketability of title. By law, all these entities have to follow strict operating standards that govern their document-tracking capabilities, physical storage facilities and staffing.

Although they are established to protect both the security of ownership and that of transactions, it is obvious that Western systems emphasize the latter. Security is principally focused on producing trust in transactions so that people can more easily make their assets lead a parallel life as capital.

In most developing countries, by contrast, the law and official agencies are trapped by early colonial and Roman law, which tilt towards protecting ownership. They have become custodians of the wishes of the dead. This may explain why the creation of capital in Western property happens so easily, and why most of the assets in developing and ex-communist countries have slipped out of the formal legal system in search of mobility.

The Western emphasis on the security of transactions allows citizens to move large amounts of assets with very few transactions. How else can we explain that in developing and former communist nations people are still taking their pigs to market and trading them one at a time, as they have done for thousands of years, while in the West traders take representations of their rights over pigs to the market? Traders at the Chicago commodities exchange, for example, deal through representations, which give them more information about the pigs they are trading than if they could physically examine each pig. They are able to make deals for huge quantities of pigs with little concern about the security of transactions.

Capital and Money

The six effects of an integrated property process mean that Westerners' houses no longer merely keep the rain and cold out. Endowed with representational existence, these houses can now lead a parallel life, doing *economic* things they could not have done before. A well-integrated legal property system in essence does two things: first, it tremendously reduces the costs of knowing the economic qualities of assets by representing them in a way that our senses can pick up quickly; and, second, it facilitates the capacity to agree on how to use assets to create further production and increase the division of labour. The genius of the West was to have created a system that allowed people to grasp with the mind values that human eyes could never see and to manipulate things that hands could never touch.

Centuries ago, scholars speculated that we use the word 'capital' (from the Latin for 'head') because the head is where we hold the tools with which we create capital. This suggests that the reason why capital has always been shrouded in mystery is because, like energy, it can be discovered and managed only with the mind. The only way to touch capital is if the property system can record its economic aspects on paper and anchor them to a specific location and owner.

Property, then, is not mere paper but a mediating device that captures and stores most of the stuff required to make a market economy run. Property seeds the system by making people accountable and assets fungible, by tracking transactions, and so providing all the mechanisms required for the monetary and banking system to work and for investment to function. The connection between capital and modern money runs through property.

Today it is documented information that can ultimately be traced back to legal records of property ownership and transactions that provide monetary authorities with the indicators they need to issue legal tender. As cognitive scientists George A. Miller and Philip N. Johnson-Laird wrote in 1976: 'Paper currency owes its origins to the writing of debt notes. [Therefore,] money . . . presupposes the institution of property.'[9] It is property documentation that fixes the economic characteristics of assets so that they can be used to secure commercial and financial transactions, and ultimately provides the justification against which central banks issue money. To create credit and generate investment, what people encumber are not the physical assets themselves, but their property representations – the recorded titles or shares – governed by rules that can be enforced nationwide. Money does not earn money. You need a property right before you can make money. Even if you loan money, the only way you can earn on it is by loaning or investing it against some kind of property document that establishes your rights to principal and interests. To repeat: money presupposes property.

As the eminent German economists Gunnar Heinsohn and Otto Steiger point out, 'Money is *never created ex nihilo* from the point of view of property, which must always exist *before* money can come into existence.'[10] Recognizing similarities between their work and mine, they brought to my attention an unpublished draft of an article stating 'that interest and money cannot be understood without the institution of property'.[11] This relationship is obscured, they maintain, by the common misapprehension that central banks issue notes and support the ability of commercial banks to make payments. In Heinsohn and Steiger's view, what escapes the naked eye is 'that all advances are made in good banking against securities',[12] or, in my terms, legal property paper. They agree with Harold Demsetz that the property rights foundation of capitalism has been taken for granted, and note that Joseph Schumpeter already had an inkling that it is property rights that secure the creation of money. As Tom Bethell correctly states in his extraordinary book *The Noblest Triumph*: 'the many blessings of a private property system have never been properly analyzed'.[13]

Capital, as I argued earlier, is therefore not created by money; it is created by people whose property systems help them to cooperate and think about how they can get the assets they accumulate to deploy additional production. The substantial increase of capital in the West over the last two centuries is the consequence of gradually improving property systems, which allowed economic agents to discover and realize the potential in their assets, and thus to be in a position to produce the non-inflationary money with which to finance and generate additional production.

So, we are more than squirrels who store food for winter and engage in deferred consumption. We know, through the sophisticated use of property institutions, how to give the things we accumulate a parallel life. When advanced nations pulled together all the information and rules about their known assets and established property systems that tracked their economic evolution, they gathered into one order the whole institutional process that underpins the creation of capital. If capitalism had a mind, it would be located in the legal property system. But, like most things pertaining to the mind, much of 'capitalism' today operates at a subconscious level.

Why did the classical economists, who knew capital was abstract and had to be fixed, not make the connection between capital and property? One explanation may be that in Adam Smith's or even Marx's day property systems were still restricted and undeveloped and their importance was difficult to gauge. Perhaps more significantly, the battle for the future of capitalism shifted from the book-lined studies of theoreticians into a vast web of entrepreneurs, financiers, politicians and jurists. The attention of the world turned from theories to the real deals being made on the ground, day by day, fiscal year after fiscal year.

Once the vast machine of capitalism was firmly in place and its masters were busy creating wealth, the question of how it all came into being lost its urgency. Like people living in the rich and fertile delta of a long river, the advocates of capitalism had no pressing need to explore upstream for the source of their prosperity. Why bother? With the end of the Cold War, however, capitalism became the only serious option for development. So the rest of the world turned to the West for help and was advised to imitate the conditions of life on the delta: stable currencies, open markets and private businesses, the objectives of so-called 'macroeconomic and structural adjustment reforms'. Everyone forgot that the reason for the delta's rich life lay far upriver, in its unexplored headwaters. Widely accessible legal property systems are the silt from upriver that permits modern capital to flourish.

This is one of the principal reasons why macroeconomic reforms are not working. Imitating capitalism at the level of the delta, by importing McDonald's and Blockbuster franchises, is not enough to create wealth. Capital is needed, and this requires a complex and mighty system of legal property that we have all taken for granted.

Braudel's Bell Jar

Much of the marginalization of the poor in developing and former communist nations comes from their inability to benefit from the six effects that property provides. The challenge these countries face is not whether they should produce or receive more money but whether they can understand the legal institutions and summon the political will necessary to build a property system that is easily accessible to the poor.

The French historian Fernand Braudel found it a great mystery that, at its inception, Western capitalism served only a privileged few, just as it does elsewhere in the world today:

> The key problem is to find out why that sector of society of the past, which I would not hesitate to call capitalist, should have lived as if in a bell jar, cut off from the rest; why was it not able to expand and conquer the whole of society? . . . [Why was it that] a significant rate of capital formation was possible only in certain sectors and not in the whole market economy of the time? . . . It would perhaps be teasingly paradoxical to say that whatever else was in short supply, money certainly was not . . . so this was an age where poor land was bought up and magnificent country residences built, great monuments erected and cultural extravagance financed . . . [How do we] resolve the contradiction . . . between the depressed economic climate and the splendors of Florence under Lorenzo the Magnificent?[14]

I believe the answer to Braudel's question lies in restricted access to formal property, both in the West's past and in developing and former communist countries today. Local and foreign investors do have capital; their assets are more or less integrated, fungible, networked and protected by formal property systems. But they are only a tiny minority – those who can afford the expert lawyers, insider connections and patience required to navigate the red tape of their property systems. The great majority of people, who cannot get the fruits of their labour represented by the formal property system, live outside Braudel's bell jar.

The bell jar makes capitalism a private club, open only to a privileged few, and enrages the billions standing outside looking in. This capitalist apartheid will inevitably continue until we all come to terms with the critical flaw in many countries' legal and political systems that prevents the majority from entering the formal property system.

The time is right to discover why most countries have not been able to create open formal property systems. This is the moment, as Third World and ex-communist nations are living through their most ambitious attempts to implement capitalist systems, to lift the bell jar.

But before we answer that question, we have to solve the rest of the mystery of why governments have been so slow to realize that a bell jar exists.

4

THE MYSTERY OF POLITICAL AWARENESS

> *Hark, hark! the dogs do bark,*
> *The beggars are coming to town;*
> *Some in rags and some in jags,*
> *And some in silken gown.*
> *English nursery rhyme*

The breakdown of population patterns and mandatory law has been an unmistakable trend in developing countries for the past forty years and in ex-communist countries for the past ten. Since Deng Xiaoping's economic reforms began in 1979, 100 million Chinese have left their official homes in search of extralegal jobs. Three million illegal migrants besieging Beijing have created a jumble of sweatshops on the outskirts of the city. Port-au-Prince has grown fifteen times larger; Guayaquil eleven times larger; and Cairo four times larger. The underground market now accounts for 50 per cent of GDP in Russia and Ukraine and a whopping 62 per cent in Georgia. The International Labour Organization reports that since 1990 85 per cent of all new jobs in Latin America and the Caribbean have been created in the extralegal sector. In Zambia, only 10 per cent of the workforce is legally employed.

What are these countries doing about this? Quite a lot. They have rolled up their sleeves and gone to work, addressing each of these problems individually. In August 1999, for example, Bangladeshi authorities demolished fifty thousand shanties in the capital city of Dhaka. Where demolition is impossible, governments have built schools and pavements for the millions of squatters invading public and private lands. At the same time governments have supported micro-finance programmes to assist the sweatshops that are transforming residential areas into industrial zones throughout the world. They have improved the stalls of pavement vendors clogging their streets; removed hordes of drifters from their city squares and planted flowers instead; tightened construction and safety codes to prevent buildings collapsing as they did in Turkey during the 1999 earthquake. Governments have tried to force the independent jitneys and shabby taxis that glut traffic to meet minimum safety standards; they are cracking down on theft and loss of water and electricity and trying to enforce patents and copyrights. They have arrested and executed as many gangsters and drug traffickers as possible (at least the more famous ones) and jailed them (at least for a while); they have tightened security measures to control the influence of extreme political sects among the uprooted and vulnerable multitudes.

Each of these problems has its own academic speciality to study it and its own political programme to cope with it. Few seem to realize that what we have here is *one* huge, worldwide industrial revolution: a gigantic movement away from life organized on a small scale to life organized on a large one. For better or for worse, people outside the West are fleeing self-sufficient and isolated societies in an effort to raise their standards of living by becoming interdependent in much larger markets.

It is understood all too rarely that the Third World and former communist societies are experiencing nearly the same industrial revolution that arrived in the West more than two centuries ago. The difference is that this new revolution is roaring ahead much faster and transforming the lives of many more people. Britain supported just 8 million people when it began its 250-year progression from the farm to the laptop computer. Indonesia is making that same journey in only four decades and carrying a population of more than 200 million. No wonder its institutions have been slow to adapt. But adapt they must. A tide of humanity has moved from isolated communities and households to participate in ever-widening circles of economic and intellectual exchange. It is this tide that has transformed Jakarta, Mexico City, São Paolo, Nairobi, Bombay, Shanghai and Manila into mega-cities of 10, 20, 30 million and overwhelmed their political and legal institutions.

The failure of the legal order to keep pace with this astonishing economic and social upheaval has forced the new migrants to invent extralegal substitutes for established law. Whereas all manner of anonymous business transactions are widespread in advanced countries, the migrants in the developing world can deal only with people they know and trust. Such informal, *ad hoc* business arrangements do not work very well. The wider the market, as Adam Smith pointed out, the more minute the division of labour can be. And as labour grows more specialized, the economy grows more efficient and wages and capital values rise. A legal failure that prevents enterprising people from negotiating with strangers defeats the division of labour and fastens would-be entrepreneurs to smaller circles of specialization and to low productivity.

Entrepreneurship triumphed in the West because the law integrated everyone under one system of property, giving them the means to cooperate and produce large amounts of surplus value in an expanded market. The advances of the West, right up to today's exponential growth of electronic information and telecommunications technology, could happen only because the property rights systems required to make them work were already in place. Integrated legal property systems destroyed most closed groups while inviting the creation of a larger network where the potential to create capital increased substantially. In this sense, property obeys what is known as

'Metcalfe's Law' (named after Bob Metcalfe, the inventor of the Ethernet Standard that commonly networks personal computers). According to Metcalfe's Law,

> The value of a network – defined as its utility to a population – is roughly proportional to the number of users squared. An example is the telephone network. One telephone is useless: whom do you call? Two telephones are better, but not much. It is only when most of the population has a telephone that the power of the network reaches its full potential to change society.[1]

Like computer networks, which had existed for years before anyone thought to link them, property systems become tremendously powerful when they are interconnected in a larger network. Only then is the potential of a particular property right not limited to the imagination of its owner, his neighbours or his acquaintances, but subject to a larger network of other imaginations. Only then will people subject themselves to obeying one legal code because they will realize that without that code they will cease to prosper. Only then can government begin to administer development instead of heroically rushing to plug each and every leak. A modern government and a market economy are unviable without an integrated formal property system. Many of the problems of non-Western markets today are due mainly to the fragment-ation of their property arrangements and the unavailability of standard norms that allow assets and economic agents to inter-act and governments to rule by law.

When migrants move from developing and ex-communist countries to advanced nations, well-developed institutions eventually absorb them into a networked property system that helps them produce surplus value. The people who migrate within their own countries are not being accommodated in this way – at least not quickly enough. Poorer countries lack the institutions to integrate the migrants into the formal sector, fix their assets into fungible forms, make their owners account-able agents and provide them with connecting and leveraging devices that allow them to interface productively and generate capital within a large legal market. So the migrants invent, at the expense of the legal order, a variety of extralegal arrange-ments to substitute for the laws and institutions they need to cooperate in an expanded market.

Political blindness, therefore, consists of being unaware that the growth of the extralegal sector and the breakdown of the existing legal order are ultimately due to a gigantic movement away from life organized on a small scale towards one organized in a larger context. What national leaders are miss-ing is that people are spontaneously organizing themselves into separate, extralegal groups until government can provide them with one legal property system.

The fundamental problem for non-Western nations is not that people are moving to urban centres, that garbage is piling up, that infrastructure is insufficient or that the countryside is being abandoned. All of that happened in advanced nations. Nor is the problem simply urban growth. Los Angeles has grown faster than Calcutta in this century, and Tokyo is three times bigger than Delhi. The primary problem is the delay in recognizing that most of the disorder occurring outside the West is the result of a revolutionary movement that is more full of promise than of problems. Once the potential value of the movement is harnessed, many of its problems will be easier to resolve. Developing and former communist nations must choose either to create systems that allow their governments to adapt to the continual changes in the revolutionary division of labour or to continue to live in extralegal confusion – and that really isn't much of a choice.

Why has everyone missed the real problem? Because there are two blind spots. First, most of us do not see that the surge in the world's extralegal populations over the past forty years has generated a new class of entrepreneurs with their own legal arrangements. Government authorities see only a massive influx of people, illegal workers, the threat of disease and crime. So while the Housing Ministry deals with its own issues and the Ministries of Health and Justice focus on theirs, no one notices that the real cause of the disorder is not population or urban growth, or even a poor minority, but an outmoded system of legal property.

Most of us are like the six blind men in the presence of an elephant: one grasps the animal's searching trunk and thinks the elephant is a snake; another finds its tail and thinks the elephant is a rope; a third is fascinated by the large, sail-like ears; another embraces its leg and concludes that the elephant is a tree. No one views the elephant in its totality, and thus they cannot come up with a strategy for dealing with the very large problem at hand. As we have seen, the poor in developing and ex-communist countries constitute two-thirds of the world's population – and they have no alternative but to live outside the law. As we also saw, the poor have plenty of things, but their property rights are not defined by any law. The millions of enterprising people who fill 85 per cent of all new jobs in Latin America, those 3 million Chinese outside Beijing operating illegal sweatshops and those Russians who generate half of their nation's GDP are doing so on the basis of extralegal arrangements. More often than not, these grassroots property arrangements openly contradict the official, written law. That is the elephant before us.

I do not believe the appearance of small enclaves of prosperous economic sectors in the midst of large undeveloped or informal sectors marks the dawn of an uneven but nevertheless inevitable transition to capitalist systems. Rather, the existence of prosperous enclaves in a sea of poverty conceals an abysmal retardation in a nation's capacity to create, respect and make available formal property rights to the majority of its citizens.

The second blind spot is that few recognize that the problems they face are not new. The migration and extralegality plaguing cities in the developing and former communist world closely resemble what the advanced nations of the West went through during their own industrial revolution. They too focused on trying to solve their problems one by one. The lesson of the West is that piecemeal solutions and stopgap measures to alleviate poverty were not enough. Living standards rose only when governments reformed the law and the property system to facilitate the division of labour. With the ability to increase their productivity through the beneficial effects of integrated property systems, ordinary people were able to specialize in ever-widening markets and to increase capital formation.

BLIND SPOT I:
Life outside the Bell Jar Today

Why didn't we see this new industrial revolution coming? Back in the 1980s, when my colleagues and I in Peru began our work, most officials assumed that our part of the world was to a great extent controlled by law. Latin America had a long, refined and well-respected legal tradition. To be sure, there were poor people holding jobs and property outside the law, but this extralegal sector was considered relatively small and thus a 'marginal' issue. Advanced nations had their share of poverty, unemployment and black markets, and we had ours. Dealing with them was a job mainly for the police or the handful of academic sociologists who had devoted their careers to studying homegrown exotica. At best, the poor made good copy for *National Geographic* and the Discovery Channel.

But no one had any exact data. No one even knew how to measure what the poor were doing or precisely how much they owned. And so my colleagues and I decided to put away our books and academic journals, not to mention our reams of government statistics and maps, and visit the real experts on this problem: the poor themselves. Once we went into the streets to look around and listen, we began stumbling across surprising facts. For instance, the Peruvian construction industry was in a slump. Building was down, workers were being laid off. Curiously, however, at outlets for construction materials the cash registers were still ringing and sales of cement were up; *bags* of cement, that is. After further investigation, we discovered that the poor were buying more cement than ever for their construction projects – houses, buildings and businesses that were not legally registered or titled and therefore never made it on to the computer screens of the government economists and statisticians. We began to sense a vibrant, independent, officially invisible extralegal economy buzzing in the cities throughout the developing world. In Brazil, for example, the construction industry reported a mere 0.1 percent growth in 1995; yet cement sales during the first six months of 1996 soared by nearly 20 per cent. The reason for the apparent anomaly, according to a Deutsche Morgan Grenfell analysis, was that 60 to 70 per cent of the region's construction never makes it into the records.[2]

The extralegal sector, we realized, was hardly a small issue. It was *enormous*.

Growing Cities

The movement towards the cities ballooned in the 1960s for most developing countries, and in the 1980s for China. For various reasons, self-reliant communities abandoned their isolation and began trying to integrate in and around cities. Since the 1980s, millions of Chinese peasants have been illegally clustering around cities to the point where the *Beijing Youth Daily* proclaimed that 'the management of the migrant population is out of control'.[3]

The phenomenon is also familiar to countries around the Mediterranean. According to Henry Boldrick, after the Second World War, rural migrants in Turkey headed towards the cities, building their own dwellings on government land. These spontaneous settlements, known as *gecekondus*, now house at least half of Turkey's urban population. Although some *gecekondus* have been at least partly legalized and consequently have been able to gain some municipal services, the majority are still informal.[4]

In the Philippines the newspaper *Business World* called on the government 'to stem the tide of humanity that is congesting our city to bursting point . . . You see *barong-barongs* made of concrete and hollow blocks – and you begin to wonder. What is the government doing about the growing problem of homelessness, of squatters in our cities?'[5]

In South Africa some observers (including myself) believe the extralegal real estate sector is on the verge of its second major expansion. In 1998 *Newsweek* reported that 'more and more [South African blacks] are filling the squatter camps and shantytowns that surround every South African city. Under apartheid, racial pass laws confined many blacks to rural areas. Now they travel freely – but hardly in comfort.'[6] *The Economist* confirmed the trend: 'Though anti-white political violence never really materialized, the end of racial segregation made it easier for poor blacks to wander into rich white areas.'[7]

In Egypt intellectuals and technocrats seem to have been aware of the issue for some time. According to one recent report, between 1947 and 1989 'Egypt's total urban population has . . . increased . . . from 6.2 million to 23.46 million.'[8] Figures compiled by Gerard Barthelemy show that the population in the metropolitan area of Port-au-Prince, Haiti, rose from 140,000 in 1950 to 1,550,000 in 1988 and is now approaching 2 million. Barthelemy estimates that about two-thirds of these people live in shanty towns, or what the Haitians call *bidonvilles*.[9]

In Mexico the private sector has become increasingly conscious of the extralegal phenomenon and actively involved in doing something about it. According to one news report:

A 1987 study by the Center for Private Sector Economic Studies (CPSEIS) estimated that the informal sector generated economic activity worth between 28% and 39% of the official Mexican GDP, and a 1993 study . . . put the number of people in the 'non-registered informal sector' at 8 million out of a total work force of 23 million . . . 'For every formal business, there are two informal businesses,' says Antonio Montiel Guerrero, president of the Mexico City Small Business Chamber of Commerce (CANACOPE), a group representing 167,000 small, registered formal businesses. 'In the Federal District (Mexico City) there are about 350,000 small, informal businesses for a total population of roughly 8 million.' What that translates into for the whole 20-million-person Mexico City metropolitan area is anybody's guess, especially when the unregulated and growing shantytowns are concentrated outside the central core of the city.[10]

Extralegal zones in developing countries are characterized by modest homes cramped together on city perimeters, myriad workshops in their midst, armies of vendors hawking their wares on the streets, and countless crisscrossing minibus lines. All seem to have sprung out of nowhere. Steady streams of small craftsworkers, tools under their arms, have expanded the range of activities carried out in the city. Ingenious local adaptations add to the production of essential goods and services, dramatically transforming certain areas of manufacturing, retail distribution, building and transportation. The passive landscapes that once surrounded Third World cities have become the latest extensions of the metropolis, and cities modelled on the European style have yielded to a more noisy, local personality blended with drab imitations of suburban America's commercial strip.

The sheer size of most of these cities creates its own opportunities. New business owners have emerged who, unlike their predecessors, are of very humble origins. Upward mobility has increased. The patterns of consumption and exclusive luxuries of the old urban society have been displaced by other, more widespread ones.

The March to the Cities

Migration is, of course, the key factor in urban growth in most developing and ex-communist nations. Its causes, however, are hard to pinpoint. Commentators in each country offer various explanations: a war, an agrarian reform programme, the lack of agrarian reform, a foreign embargo on international trade, the opening of international trade, terrorism and guerrillas, moral decay, failed capitalism, failed socialism, even bad taste (it is so much prettier in the countryside, why don't they just stay there?).

Lately, however, opinion has been converging around a few general causes. The most visible explanation for the wave in migration throughout the developing world is better roads. The building of roads and bridges and the transformation of unconnected paths into proper highways awakened the rural population to the possibility of travel, and they began moving to the cities. New means of communication provided an additional incentive. Radio, in particular, aroused expectations of increased consumption and income. From thousands of miles away came radio broadcasts publicizing the opportunities, amenities and comforts of urban life. Modernity sounded within reach of anyone with the courage to head down the road after it.

There is also now fairly widespread agreement that agricultural crises in many countries were other decisive factors. The modernization of agriculture and the uncertain market for some traditional crops following the Second World War triggered massive layoffs of farm labourers on traditional estates and unleashed vast contingents of people prepared to search for new horizons.

There was also the problem of property rights in the

countryside. The long, complex process of agrarian reform only compounded – and ultimately exacerbated – the traditional difficulties of acquiring land suitable for farming. Unable to own land or find work in the countryside, many people migrated to the cities.

Another powerful attraction was the lower infant mortality rate in most principal cities. This gap between infant mortality in the cities and rural areas widened as medical services in the cities began improving after the Second World War. Better wages were also an important incentive. In Latin America, for example, by 1970 people leaving the countryside to take up semi-skilled employment in capital cities could double or triple their monthly income. A salaried job might quadruple their previous income, and professionals or technicians could earn six times as much. Higher pay offset the risk of un-employment: a migrant who had been unemployed for a year could recoup the lost income in two and a half months in the city. Life in the far-off cities not only seemed better; it was better.

Even the growth of national bureaucracies became an incentive for migration. The centralization of power in the hands of government officials meant that most of the government offices competent to provide advice, answer requests, issue permits or provide jobs were located in the cities. And any migrant seeking a brighter future for his children knew that the opportunities for education were much better in the cities. To underemployed peasants with few resources other than their own ingenuity, education was an increasingly valuable and productive investment. Cities contained most of the secondary school graduates as well as students enrolled in vocational training centres, schools and institutes of higher education, and university applicants and entrants.

Migration, therefore, is hardly an irrational act. It has little to do with 'herd instinct'. It is the product of a calculated, rational assessment by rural people of their current situation measured against the opportunities open to them elsewhere.

Rightly or wrongly, they believed that migrating to larger markets would benefit them. The move, however, was not an easy one.

Poor People Go Home

Migrants to the cities encountered a hostile world. They soon realized that, while urban people had a romantic, even tender image of the farmers and were quick to acknowledge that all citizens had a right to happiness, they preferred that the good farmers pursue their happiness at home. Peasants were not supposed to come looking for modernity. To that end, virtually every country in the developing and ex-communist world maintained development programmes to bring modernity to the countryside.

The greatest hostility toward migrants came from the legal system. At first, the system could easily absorb or ignore them because the small groups who had arrived were hardly likely to upset the status quo. As their numbers grew, however, to the point where they could no longer be ignored, newcomers found themselves barred from legally established social and economic activities. It was tremendously difficult for them to get access to housing, enter formal business or find a legal job. The legal institutions of most Third World countries had been developed over the years to serve the needs and interests of certain urban groups; dealing with the peasants in rural areas was a separate matter. As long as the peasants stayed put, the implicit legal discrimination was not apparent. Once they settled in the cities, however, they experienced the apartheid of formal law. Suddenly, the bell jar was visible.

Some of the nations of the former Soviet Union also face disarray in their property systems, and at least some élites are recognizing the economic benefits of sorting it out. According to a 1996 report,

Mechanisms . . . to protect land rights are in their infancy in
Russia . . . In many regions land must be registered with an
agency distinct from the one that registers buildings. Moreover,
the legal protections that registration provides are unclear . . .
Procedures and customs for protection and use of land rights
must be created from scratch . . . Land is probably Russia's
most valuable resource, a resource upon which an entire economy and a democratic society can be based.'[11]

We have found that throughout the Third World, extralegal
activities burgeon whenever the legal system imposes rules that
thwart the expectations of those it excludes. As we saw in
Chapter 2, many countries make the obstacles to entering the
legal property systems so daunting and expensive that few
migrants could ever make their way through the red tape – as
many as 14 years and 77 bureaucratic procedures at 31 public
and private agencies in Egypt, and 19 years and 176 bureaucratic steps to legalize the purchase of private land in Haiti.

If there are costs to becoming legal, there are also bound to
be costs to remaining outside the law. We found that operating
outside the world of legal work and business was surprisingly
expensive. In Peru, for example, the cost of operating a
business extralegally includes paying 10 to 15 per cent of its
annual income in bribes and commissions to authorities. Add
to such payoffs the costs of avoiding penalties, making transfers outside legal channels and operating from dispersed
locations and without credit, and the life of the extralegal
entrepreneur turns out to be far more costly and full of daily
hassles than that of the legal businessman.

Perhaps the most significant cost was caused by the absence
of institutions that create incentives for people to seize
economic and social opportunities to specialize within the
market place. We found that people who could not operate
within the law also could not hold property efficiently or
enforce contracts through the courts; nor could they reduce

uncertainty through limited liability systems and insurance policies, or create stock companies to attract additional capital and share risk. Being unable to raise money for investment, they could not achieve economies of scale or protect their innovations through royalties and patents.

Blocked from entering the bell jar, the poor could never get close to the legal property mechanisms necessary to generate capital. The disastrous economic effects of this legal apartheid are most strikingly visible in the lack of formal property rights over real estate. In every country we researched we found that some 80 per cent of land parcels were not protected by up-to-date records or held by legally accountable owners. Any exchange of such extralegal property was therefore restricted to closed circles of trading partners, keeping the assets of extralegal owners outside the expanded market.

Extralegal asset owners are thus denied access to the credit that would allow them to expand their operations — an essential step towards starting or growing a business in advanced countries. In the United States, for example, up to 70 per cent of the credit new businesses receive comes from using formal titles as collateral for mortgages. Extralegality also means that the incentives for investment provided by legal security are missing.

Cut off from the legal system, the migrants' only guarantee of prosperity lay in their own hands. They had to compete not only against other people but against the system itself. If the legal systems of their own countries were not going to welcome them, they had no alternative but to set up their own extralegal systems. These extralegal systems, in my opinion, constitute the most important rebellion against the status quo in the history of developing countries since their independence, and in the countries of the former Soviet bloc since the collapse of communism.

Growing Extralegality

The populations of most major Third World cities have shown fourfold increase in the past four decades. By 2015 over fifty cities in developing countries will have 5 million or more people,[12] with most living and working extralegally. The extralegal sector is omnipresent in the developing and former communist countries. New activities have emerged and gradually replaced traditional ones. Walk down most streets and you are bound to bump into extralegal shops, currency exchange, transport and other services. Even many of the books for sale have been printed extralegally.

Entire neighbourhoods have been acquired, developed and built on the fringes of, or in direct opposition to, government regulations by extralegal settlements and businesses. Of every hundred homes built in Peru, only about thirty have legal title; seventy have been built extralegally. Throughout Latin America, we found, at least six out of eight buildings were in the undercapitalized sector, and 80 per cent of all real estate was held *outside* the law. According to most estimates, the extralegal sectors in the developing world account for 50 to 75 per cent of all working people and are responsible for one-fifth to more than two-thirds of the total economic output of the Third World.

Consider Brazil: as we have seen, thirty years ago, more than two-thirds of housing construction was for rent; today rentals constitute scarcely 3 per cent of Brazil's construction. Most of that market has moved to the informal parts of Brazilian cities – the *favelas*. According to Donald Stewart:

> People are not conscious of the volume of economic activity that exists in a *favela*. These informal economies were born of the entrepreneurial spirit of peasants from the North East of Brazil that were attracted by urban centers. They operate outside the highly regulated formal economy and function according to supply and demand. In spite of the apparent lack

of resources, this informal economy functions efficiently. In the *favelas* there are no rent controls, rents are paid in US dollars and renters who do not pay are rapidly evicted. The profitability of investment is good and as a result there is an abundance of supply of housing. [13]

The *Wall Street Journal* reported in 1997 that, according to the group Friends of the Land, only 10 per cent of land occupied in the Brazilian Amazon jungle is covered by property titles.[14] In other countries extralegality is on the rise.

Unlike the situation in advanced nations, where the 'underclass' represents a small minority living on the margin of society, in some countries extralegality has always been the mainstream. For example, in most countries we have surveyed, the value of extralegal real estate alone is many times greater than total savings and time deposits in commercial banks, the value of companies registered in local stock exchanges, all foreign direct investment and all public enterprises privatized and to be privatized put together. This should not, on reflection, be surprising: real estate accounts for some 50 per cent of the national wealth of advanced nations; in developing countries the figure is closer to three-quarters. Extralegal settlements are often the only avenue for investment in developing and ex-communist countries and therefore represent an important part of the savings and capital formation process. Moreover, the growing contribution of cities to GNP suggests that a great deal of potential capital and technological know-how is being accumulated mainly in urban areas.

The Extralegals Have Come to Stay

This explosion of extralegal activity in the Third World, the massive squatting in rural areas and the sprawling illegal cities – Peru's *pueblos jóvenes*, Brazil's *favelas*, Venezuela's *ranchos*, Mexico's *barrios marginales* and the *bidonvilles* of the ex-

French colonies as well as the shanty towns of the former British ones – is much more than a surge of population, or poverty, or even illegality. These waves of extralegals crashing up against the bell jars of legal privilege could very well be the most important factor forcing authorities to welcome the industrial and commercial revolution that is upon them.

Most governments in most nations are in no condition to compete with extralegal power. In strictly physical terms extralegal ventures have already overtaken government efforts to provide housing for migrants and the poor. In Peru until the end of the 1980s, for example, government investment in low-income housing hovered around 2 per cent of the housing investment in the extralegal sector. Including middle-class housing raised the government share to only 10 per cent of total informal investments. In Haiti in 1995 the value of extralegal real estate was nearly ten times greater than all the holdings of the Haitian government.

This extralegal sector is a grey area that has a long frontier with the legal world, a place where individuals take refuge when the cost of obeying the law outweighs the benefit. The migrants became extralegals to survive: they stepped outside the law because they were not allowed inside. In order to live, trade, manufacture, transport or even consume, the cities' new inhabitants had to do so extralegally.

The extralegal arrangements they cobbled together are explicit obligations between certain members of society to provide security for their property and activities. They represent combinations of rules selectively borrowed from the official legal system, *ad hoc* improvisations and customs brought from their places of origin or locally devised, and they are held together by a social contract supported by the community as a whole and enforced by authorities the community has selected. The disadvantage to extralegal arrangements is that they are not integrated into the formal property system and as a result are not fungible and adaptable to most transactions; they are not connected into the financial and investment circuit; and their members are not accountable to authorities outside their own social contract.

These arrangements are run by a large variety of organizations, including urban development associations, farming conventions, small merchant associations, small business organizations, micro-entrepreneurial communities, transport federations, miners' claim clubs, agrarian reform beneficiaries, private housing cooperatives, settlement organizations, residential boards, communal committees, beneficiary committees in state-built housing, native communities, small farmers' associations and village organizations. These organizations result from different types of extralegal occupation, such as building extensions on desert land, building extensions on agricultural land, special arrangements for historic parts of the cities, subdivisions of public housing, settlements with private contracts, settlements with public contracts, appropriations through subleasing with owner's consent, state housing with incomplete titling, illegal tenancy contracts declared before a notary and not recorded, settlement contracts recorded but not declared before a notary, settlements recognized by 'national peace processes', relocated settlers, settlements recorded with suppliers of basic services or tax authorities but not recorded with the official property custodians.

Extralegality is rarely antisocial in intent. The 'crimes' extralegals commit are designed to achieve such ordinary goals as building a house, providing a service or developing a business. Far from being the cause of disarray, this system of extralegal law is the only way settlers have to regulate their lives and transactions. As a result, nothing could be more socially relevant to the way the poor live and work. While their 'laws' may be outside formal law, they are, by and large, the only laws with which these people are comfortable. This is the social contract by which they live and work.

The extralegal settlements the migrants inhabit may look like slums, but they are quite different from the inner-city slums of advanced nations. The latter consist of once-decent buildings falling apart from neglect and poverty. In the developing world the basic shelters of the poor are likely to be improved, built up and progressively gentrified. While the houses of the poor in advanced nations lose value over time, the buildings in the poor settlements of the developing world become more valuable, evolving within decades into the equivalent of working-class communities in the West.

Above all, the extralegal settlers, contrary to their lawless image, share the desire of civil society to lead peaceful, productive lives. As Simon Fass wrote in the eloquent conclusion of his book about the economy of Haiti,

> These ordinary people are extraordinary in only one respect. Their incomes are very low, so low that one serious error of judgment or one unfortunate act of providence can often threaten survival of a household as a corporate entity, and sometimes also threaten survival of its members as corporeal entities. What is extraordinary is not so much the poverty itself, but rather the ability of these people to survive in spite of it . . . Nothing they do in this process is anything but a productive contribution to survival and growth, and the simple items they obtain have concrete functions as factor inputs to the production process.[15]

As the economic activities with which they are associated have grown and diversified, these extralegal organizations have also begun to assume the role of government. To varying degrees, they have become responsible for the provision of such basic infrastructure as roads, water supply, sewage systems and electricity, the construction of markets, the provision of transport services and even the administration of justice and the maintenance of order.

In the face of the extralegals' advance governments have retreated. But they are inclined to consider each concession temporary, 'until the crisis has passed'. In reality, however, this strategy is only a way of delaying the inevitable defeat. In some cases governments have created exceptions for some extralegal enterprises, legal enclaves as it were, where originally illegal enterprises can operate without persecution – but without integrating them so that they enjoy the protection and benefits of the entire legal system. These arrangements avoid open confrontation and as such can be considered a sort of transitory legal peace treaty. In Egypt, for example, experts are already talking about 'semi-formal housing':

> Such housing not only increases the housing stock within the country and provides relatively cheap housing but also provides a large proportion of the urban population with an asset in which they can invest. This kind of housing does have some degree of illegality. The housing structures are not developed through established, regulated procedures and those who construct them do not use the recognized institutions of housing. They are usually constructed on agricultural areas which were illegally sub-divided into small plots by the private developers . . .
>
> The government is usually involved in the process of land acquisition within semi-informal housing. In the semi-formal housing areas where the research was undertaken, it was government bodies that initiated their development and this encouraged private developers to sub-divide the land illegally into small plots at a later stage. Land use was changed from agricultural to residential use through a covert role from the government. The inhabitants within such areas usually acquire their land through an informal process of sub-division and informal land commercialization. Hager El Mawatayah, Exbet Abou Soliman and Ezbet Nadi El Sid are the best examples of such areas in the city of Alexandria.[16]

Even in the most unlikely places, there is evidence that governments are recognizing that their legal institutions have not adapted to today's economic conditions. In 1992 Reuters reported that Libyan leader Muammar Gaddafi had incinerated Libya's land titles. 'All records and documents in the old land register, which showed that a land belonged to this or that tribe, have been burned,' Colonel Gaddafi reportedly informed a meeting of his Justice Ministry. 'They were burned because they were based on exploitation, forgery and looting.'[17]

In some countries the extralegal sector is now at the very root of the social system. The people of Touba, Senegal, who can be seen hawking their wares on the sidewalks of New York and other big US cities, are often part of a sophisticated Islamic-African sect that funnels millions of dollars of profits back to their home city. *Newsweek* describes Touba as 'A state within a state, largely exempt from Senegal's laws . . . [and] the country's fastest growing city. Entire villages have relocated here, setting up tin shacks among the walled villas of the rich . . . The duty free city is the hub of Senegal's transportation and real estate empires, the booming informal sector and the peanut trade, the nation's main source of foreign exchange.'[18]

In other parts of the world extralegals' concerns about losing their property can ignite open conflict. A case in point is Indonesia whose problems have been much in the news in recent years. As far back as six years ago, *The Economist* was warning:

> Poor people are edgy about losing their property because urbanization and industrialization are creating demand for land, in a country in which land ownership is an extremely murky business. Only 7% of the land on the Indonesian archipelago has a clear owner.
>
> Inevitably, there is a large trade in both genuine and forged certificates. People trying to buy parcels of land sometimes find numerous apparent owners. And banks are very wary of accepting land as collateral for loans.[19]

Elsewhere extralegality is closely associated with misery: 'In Bombay. . . two thirds of the city's 10 million residents live in either one-room shacks or on the pavement.'[20] Yet extralegals in other countries are moving up the economic ladder. According to the Technical Evaluations Organization of Peru (Cuerpo Técnico de Tasaciones del Perú), while the value of land in the formal sector of Lima averages some US$50 per square metre, in the area of Gamarra, where a great deal of Peru's informal manufacturing sector resides, the value per square metre can go as high as US$3,000. In Aviación, another extralegal centre in Lima, land is worth US$1,000 per square metre; and in Chimú of the Zárate section, it is US$400. By contrast, in Miraflores and San Isidro, Lima's most prestigious addresses, the value of legal, titled property ranges from US$500 to US$1,000 per square metre.[21]

It is an Old Story

Once governments understand that the poor have already taken control of vast quantities of real estate and productive economic units, it will become clear that many of the problems they confront are the result of the written law not being in harmony with the way their country actually works. It stands to reason that if the written law is in conflict with the laws citizens live by, discontent, corruption, poverty and violence are sure to follow.

The only question that remains is how soon governments will begin to legitimize these extralegal holdings by integrating them into an orderly and coherent legal framework. The alternative is perpetuating a legal anarchy in which the existing property rights system continually competes with the extralegal one. If these countries are ever to achieve a single legal system, official law must adapt to the reality of a massive extralegal push towards widespread property rights.

The good news is that legal reformers will not be stepping into an abyss. The challenge they are up against, though enormous, has been met before in many countries. Developing and ex-communist countries are facing (albeit in much more dramatic proportions) the same challenges the advanced nations dealt with between the eighteenth century and the Second World War. Massive extralegality is not a new phenomenon. It is what always happens when governments fail to make the law coincide with the way people live and work.

When the Industrial Revolution began in Europe, governments were also plagued with uncontrollable migration, growth of the extralegal sector, urban poverty and social unrest. They, too, originally addressed these problems piecemeal.

BLIND SPOT II:
Life outside Yesterday's Bell Jar

The Move to the Cities

Most writers link the coming of the great industrial and commercial revolution in Europe to the mass migrations to its cities, the growth of the population as a result of a decline in plagues, and a reduction in rural incomes compared with urban incomes.[22] In the seventeenth and eighteenth centuries workers in the cities began to receive higher wages than those in rural areas for carrying out construction projects ordered by the ruling classes. Inevitably, the more ambitious peasants migrated to the cities, enticed by the prospect of higher wages.

In England the first wave of migration began late in the sixteenth century. Disconcerted by the growing numbers of migrants in the cities and the resulting unrest, authorities tried to keep the peace with various stopgap measures such as distributing food among the poor. There were also persistent measures to persuade people to return to the countryside. A series of laws enacted in 1662, 1685 and 1693 required that citizens return to their place of birth or their previous fixed residence as a condition of receiving relief. The aim was to prevent more families and labourers from migrating to the cities in search of employment. In 1697 a law was passed allowing migrants to move about England only if they obtained a certificate of settlement from the authorities in their new place of residence. While these laws did discourage migration among families and the infirm, young, able-bodied and ambitious unmarried men devised ways of returning to the cities. They were also the sort who made successful entrepreneurs – or violent revolutionaries.

Most migrants did not find the jobs they expected. Restrictive regulations, particularly difficulties in obtaining permission to expand or diversify activities, limited the capacity of formal businesses to grow and provide jobs for new labourers. Some found temporary work or entered domestic service.[23] Many were forced to settle precariously on the outskirts of Europe's cities, in 'suburbs', the extralegal settlements of the day, awaiting admission to a guild or a job in a legal business.

Social unrest was inevitable. No sooner did the migration to the cities begin than the existing political institutions fell behind a rapidly changing reality. The rigidity of mercantilist law and custom prevented migrants from realizing their full economic potential. The overcrowding of an increasing urban population, disease and the inevitable difficulties of country people adapting to life in the city further aggravated social conflict. D. C. Coleman observes that as early as the sixteenth century there were complaints in the English Parliament about the 'multitude of beggars' and the great increase in 'rogues, vagabonds and thieves' in the cities.[24]

Instead of adapting to this new urban reality, governments created more laws and regulations to try to stamp it out. More regulations brought more infringements – and soon new laws were passed to prosecute those who broke the old ones.

Lawsuits proliferated; smuggling and counterfeiting were widespread. Governments resorted to violent repression.

The Emergence of Extralegality

Gradually, European migrants who did not find legal employment began to open illegal workshops in their homes. Much of this work 'consisted of the direct processing, with little capital equipment beyond simple hand tools'.[25] Long-time city dwellers despised the work done outside the guilds and the official industrial system.

The migrants, of course, could not afford to be choosy; extralegal work was their only source of income, and the extralegal sector of the economy began spreading rapidly. Eli Heckscher quotes a comment by Oliver Goldsmith in 1762: 'There is scarcely an Englishman who does not almost every day of his life offend with impunity some express law . . . and none but the venal and the mercenary attempt to enforce them.'[26] Two French decrees (of 1687 and 1693), also cited by Heckscher, recognized that one reason why production specifications were not being complied with was that the workers, then even more illiterate than in developing countries today, could not meet even the simple legal requirement that textile manufacturers put their names on the fore-pieces of their cloth. Still, these migrant workers were efficient. Adam Smith once remarked that 'If you would have your work tolerably executed, it must be done in the suburbs where the workmen, having no exclusive privilege, have nothing but their character to depend on, and you must then smuggle it into the town as well as you can.'[27]

Authorities and legal businessmen were not as impressed with the competition as Adam Smith. In England during the decades following the restoration of the monarchy in 1660 some traditionalists began to complain about the growing numbers of pedlars and street vendors, the disturbances that took place in front of established shops, and the appearance of new shop-keepers in many small cities. Formal traders tried in vain to get rid of the newcomers. In Paris the legal battle between tailors and secondhand-clothes dealers went on for more than three hundred years. It was stopped only by the French Revolution.

The preambles to laws and ordinances of this era frequently refer to non-compliance with previous laws and regulations. According to Heckscher, printed calicoes imported from India were prohibited in 1700 in order to protect England's woollen industry. Enterprising English manufacturers produced their own calicoes, always managing to find exceptions or loopholes in the law. One way around the ban on printing cotton-based fabrics was to use fustians – English calicoes made with a linen warp. Spain also prosecuted and punished its extralegal entrepreneurs. In 1549 Emperor Charles I promulgated twenty-five ordinances aimed at extralegal businesses. One law called for authorities to mutilate fabric samples by cutting off the selvedges containing the manufacturer's mark so that buyers would know they were purchasing extralegal goods. This was intended to humiliate distributors.

Government repression of extralegals was plentiful, harsh and, in France, deadly. In the mid-eighteenth century laws prohibiting the French public from manufacturing, importing, or selling cotton prints carried penalties ranging from slavery and imprisonment to death. The extralegals remained un-deterred. Heckscher estimates that within one ten-year period in the eighteenth century the French executed more than six-teen thousand smugglers and clandestine manufacturers for the illegal manufacture or import of printed calicoes. An even larger number were sentenced to the galleys or punished in other ways. In the town of Valence alone, 77 extralegal entrepreneurs were hanged, 58 were broken on the wheel and 631 were sentenced to the galleys. Authorities found it in their hearts to set free only one extralegal.

According to Ekelund and Tollison, the reason why the authorities prosecuted extralegals so harshly was not only because they wanted to protect established industries; multi-coloured prints also made taxes more difficult to collect.[28] Although it was easy to identify manufacturers of single-coloured textiles and thus verify whether they were paying all their taxes, calicoes, due to a new printing system, could be made with a variety of colours, making it much more difficult to identify their origin.

The state relied heavily on the guilds – whose main function was to control access to legal enterprise – to help identify law-breakers. But by making the laws more stringent instead of adjusting them to include extralegal manufacturing, the authorities simply forced entrepreneurs to the extralegal suburbs. When the English Statute of Artificers and Apprentices of 1563 fixed wage rates for workers and required that they be adjusted annually according to the prices of certain basic necessities, many of the earliest extralegals moved their businesses to outlying towns or established new suburbs where state supervision was less strict and regulations more lax or simply inapplicable. Retreating to the suburbs also allowed extralegals to escape the watchful eye of the guilds, whose jurisdiction extended only to city boundaries.

Eventually, extralegal competition increased to the point that formal business owners had no alternative but to subcontract part of their production to suburban workshops – narrowing the tax base and causing taxes to rise. A vicious circle set in: higher taxes exacerbated unemployment and unrest, prompting greater migration to the suburbs and more subcontracting to extralegal manufacturers. Some extralegals did so well that they won the right to enter formal business – though not without paying their share of bribes and applying political pressure.

The guilds fought back. Under the Tudors, numerous laws in England prohibited extralegal workshops and services in the suburbs, but the sheer number of extralegals and their skill at avoiding detection thwarted these efforts. Among the most notable failures were the hat and coverlet makers' guilds in

Norwich, which, after a protracted and highly publicized campaign against extralegal operators, were unable to enforce their exclusive legal right to manufacture hats and coverlets.[29] Competition had left the guilds reeling. Coleman attributes their decline to the 'increasing labour supply, changing patterns of demand and expanding trade; the growth of new industries and the considerable extension of rural industry organized on the putting-out system'.[30]

The Breaking Down of the Old Order

European governments were gradually forced to retreat in the face of growing extralegality – as governments in developing and ex-communist countries are doing today. In Sweden, unable to stop the establishment of extralegal settlements, King Gustavus Adolphus had to visit each settlement and give it his blessing to maintain an appearance of government control. In England the state was forced to recognize that new industries were developing primarily in places where there were no guilds or legal restrictions; indeed, extralegals had created their own suburbs and towns specifically to avoid control by the state and the guilds. Moreover, the extralegal industries were more efficient and successful. It was widely acknowledged that the cotton textile industry had boomed because it was not regulated as strictly as the woollen industry. People soon began noticing that the extralegal settlements were producing better goods and services than their legal competitors inside the bell jars. In 1588 a report to Lord Cecil, minister to Queen Elizabeth I, described the citizens of Halifax, one of the new extralegal settlements:

> They excel the rest in policy and industry, for the use of their trade and grounds and, after the rude and arrogant manner of their wild country, they surpass the rest in wisdom and wealth. They despise their old fashions if they can hear of a new, more

commodious, rather affecting novelties than allied to old cere-
monies ... [They have] a natural ardency of new inventions
annexed to an unyielding industry.[31]

Extralegals also began building within the cities. In Germany,
where it was necessary to pass a test and obtain legal approval
in order to build, according to one historian, 'whole districts
could be found in which plenty of houses were being built,
though there was no one in the district legally qualified to
build them'.[32]

The extralegals' numbers, persistence and success began to
undermine the very foundations of the mercantilist order.
Whatever success they had, it was won in spite of the state,
and they were bound to view the authorities as their enemies.
In those countries where the state outlawed and prosecuted
extralegal entrepreneurs instead of adjusting the system to
absorb their enterprise, not only was economic progress
delayed but unrest increased, spilling into violence. The best-
known manifestations were the French and Russian
revolutions.

Those countries that adapted quickly, however, made a
relatively peaceful transition to a market economy. As soon as
the state realized that a working extralegal sector was socially,
politically and economically preferable to a growing number
of unemployed migrants, authorities began withdrawing
support from the guilds. The result in England was that fewer
and fewer people applied for admission to the guilds, thereby
setting the stage for the state drastically to alter the way in
which business was conducted.

The power of the state also declined. Any legal system as
rigid as the one that preceded the Industrial Revolution was
bound to be rife with corruption. A 1692 ordinance in
England stated that tax inspectors in many areas visited workshops and factories merely to collect agreed-upon tax
payments without ever examining the goods to see how much
the producers really owed. Most production supervisors,

whether they belonged to the guilds or were appointed by the state, were continually accused of corruption and neglect of duties, a situation that was attributed to lack of civic respect for the law.

Even Members of Parliament, which by the end of the seventeenth century had the power to authorize the establishment of businesses, were known to receive bribes for special favours. Local authorities were worse. In 1601 a speaker in the House of Commons defined a justice of the peace as 'a living Creature that for half a Dozen of Chickens will Dispense with a whole Dozen of Penal Statutes'. Public officials sought to blame legislative failures not on bad laws but on inadequate enforcement. 'I conclude better laws in these points cannot be made, only there wants execution,' declared one pamphlet in 1577. Joseph Reid argues that the old order broke down because widespread corruption permeated all its institutions and divided the population into those who could outwit the system and those who could not. He also notes that a legal system that encouraged some people to break the law and made others suffer from it would inevitably lose prestige among both constituencies.[33] Suburban justices of the peace had little incentive to enforce laws that had been drafted in the cities and were unacceptable to suburban residents. By the end of the eighteenth century the entire legal apparatus had been weakened and in some countries was completely corrupt.

At a time when government controlled everything, people placed all their economic expectations in the state. This gave rise to a pattern typical of pre-capitalism: when wages went up faster than food prices, merchants called for wage ceilings; when food prices went up faster than wages, workers demanded a minimum wage and a price ceiling on foodstuffs. Prices, incomes and wages were fixed by political pressure and action, a situation that discouraged industrial and agricultural production and hiring. Neither minimum nor maximum prices, therefore, could solve the problems of scarcity, food shortages and unemployment. 'The age', writes Charles

Wilson, 'was one of violence, when the pursuit of economic ends constantly demanded the backing of force.' [34] It was a time ripe for ideological and partisan battle, in parliaments and in the streets.

As early as 1680 a kind of fatalism had emerged in the face of the apparent impossibility of substantial economic progress: 'the generality of poor manufacturers believe they shall never be worth ten pounds . . .; and if it so be they can provide for themselves sufficient to maintain their manner of living by working only three days in the week, they will never work four days'.[35]

Amid such economic crises and social unrest, the strongest and most self-confident people chose to emigrate or join revolutionary movements. Between the seventeenth and nineteenth centuries hundreds of thousands of Italians, Spaniards, French and other Europeans emigrated to other lands in search of a better future. In France the persecution of the Huguenots and the extralegals in the textile sector prompted many entrepreneurs and skilled workmen to leave, mainly for England and Holland, where they and their hosts managed to prosper.

And Finally – after 300 Years

As badly structured regulations stifled formal businesses, and as extralegals openly defied the law and voiced their dissatisfaction at being pushed to the margins, the stage was set for politicians to adapt to the facts on the ground. The law had ossified at about the same rate as the migrant settlements encircled the cities. And as pedlars, beggars and thieves invaded the streets, as extralegally manufactured or smuggled goods glutted the markets, official corruption became rampant, and violence disrupted civil society.

Law began adapting to the needs of common people, including their expectations about property rights, in most West European countries during the nineteenth and early twentieth centuries. By that time, the Europeans had concluded that it was impossible to govern the Industrial Revolution and the presence of massive extralegality through minor *ad hoc* adjustments. Politicians finally understood that the problem was not people but the law, which was discouraging and preventing people from being more productive.

Although the picture of pre-capitalist society and the circumstances of its decline are quite similar in most European countries, the outcome was not always the same. Countries that made legal efforts to integrate extralegal enterprise prospered more quickly than the countries that resisted change. By easing access to formal property, reducing the obstacles engendered by obsolete regulations and allowing existing local arrangements to influence lawmaking, European politicians eliminated the contradictions in their legal and economic systems and allowed their nations to carry the Industrial Revolution to new heights.

The past of Europe strongly resembles the present of developing and former communist countries. The fundamental problem that the latter face is not that people are invading and clogging the cities, that public services are inadequate, that garbage is piling up, that ragged children beg in the streets, or even that the benefits of macroeconomic reform programs are not reaching the majority. Many of these difficulties existed in Europe (and also the United States) and were eventually overcome. The real problem is that we have still not recognized that all these difficulties constitute a sea change in expectations: as the poor flow into cities and create extralegal social contracts they are forcing a major redistribution of power. Once the governments of developing and former communist countries accept that, they can begin to catch the wave instead of being engulfed by it.

5

THE MISSING LESSONS OF US HISTORY

This land is blessed in having to surmount only one tyranny:
that of the status quo.

MILTON AND ROSE FRIEDMAN

As I became increasingly interested in the role of formal
property systems in economic development, I made numerous
trips to advanced nations to find out how their property rights
experts would go about integrating a nation's extralegal assets
into one legal property system. After thirteen years, thousands
of miles and a little more grey hair, I had visited just about
every property-related organization in the advanced world –
from my friends in His Majesty's Land Registry and the Alaska
Land Authority to the Japanese Toki Bo. No one had an
answer. All the experts I queried, all the professionals associated with the myriad property-related institutions and agencies
I visited admitted they had never thought about the question.

People who operate property systems in advanced nations
have fundamentally different concerns. They are largely preoccupied with matters relating to property rights. My primary
concern, however, was not property rights *per se*, but 'meta-
rights' – access or rights to property rights. While we had
many subjects of mutual interest, such as how to re-engineer a

record-keeping organization so as to integrate information gathered in the field into one database, or how to develop procedures to digitize boundaries on base maps, the property experts could not tell me how to bring people who hold their assets by extralegal arrangements into the legal property system. How do you give people rights to legal property rights?

It was obvious, from what little Western history I had read, that at some point in their past all Western nations had made the transition from dispersed, informal arrangements to an integrated legal property system. So why didn't I just go there – into the history of the West to see how their property systems had evolved? My hosts agreed wholeheartedly, and the history buffs at the HM Land Registry and the German Association of Licensed Surveyors pointed me to their favourite books.

My reading, thousands of pages later, led me to the fundamental conclusion that the transition to integrated legal property systems had little to do with technology. (Although technology plays a very important supporting role, as we shall see in Chapter 6.) The crucial change had to do with adapting the law to the social and economic needs of the majority of the population. Gradually, Western nations became able both to acknowledge that social contracts born outside the official law were a legitimate source of law, and to find ways of absorbing these contracts. Law was thus made to serve popular capital formation and economic growth. This is what gives the present property institutions of the West their vitality. Moreover, this property revolution was always a *political* victory. In every country it was a result of a few enlightened men deciding that official law made no sense if a sizeable part of the population lived outside it.

The various histories of property in Western Europe, Japan and the United States all have something useful to say about the present concerns of developing and ex-communist countries. In each country apparent lawlessness was not really about crime but a collision between rule-making at the grassroots level and rule-making at the top. The revolution in each case involved the gradual merging of both systems.

However, detailed histories of all these countries would be too much for this book. I have decided, therefore, to focus on the United States because, more than 150 years ago, it too was a Third World country. The governments and judiciary of the young states, not yet so legally united, were trying to cope with the law and disorder of migrants, squatters, gold diggers, armed gangs, illegal entrepreneurs and the rest of the colourful characters who made the settling of the American West so wild and, if only in hindsight, so romantic. To a Third Worlder like me, this picture of the gringo past is astonishingly familiar. While my colleagues and I have trouble relating to 11,000 on the Dow Jones, we feel quite at home among the squatters in Thomas Jefferson's Virginia or the log cabin settlements of Daniel Boone's Kentucky.

Like Third World authorities today, American governments tried to stem the exponential increase of squatters and extra-legal arrangements; but unlike Third World authorities, they eventually conceded that, in the words of one US congressman, 'the land system is virtually broken down . . . and instead of legislating for them, we are to legislate after them in full pursuit to the Rocky Mountains or the Pacific Ocean'. What US politicians eventually learned, as Francis Philbrick put it, was that the 'forces that change the law in other than trivial ways lie outside it'.[1] Even the celebrated 'Homestead Act' of 1862, which entitled settlers to 160 acres of free land simply for agreeing to live on it and develop it, was less an act of official generosity than the recognition of a *fait accompli*: Americans had been settling —and improving— the land extralegally for decades. Their politicians gradually modified the law to integrate this reality into the official legal system, and won some political points in the bargain. Having thus changed their laws to accommodate existing extralegal arrangements, United States officials left the assets of the American settlers and miners primed to be converted into capital. As in the United States in the nineteenth century, the challenge of capitalizing the poor in the Third World and former communist countries is at bottom a political challenge that has to be reformed with legal tools.

In describing the evolution of property in the United States, as I will do in this chapter, I do not presume to rewrite the history of America; like my legendary namesake, I am simply exploring it. In the process, as you will see, I found many examples that reminded me of developing and former communist countries today: massive migrations, explosions of extralegal activity, political unrest and general discontent with an antiquated legal system that refused to acknowledge that its doctrines and formulas had little relevance to the real world. I also found how US law gradually integrated extralegal arrangements to bring about a peaceful order – thereby demonstrating, as we shall see in Chapter 6, that the law must be compatible with how people arrange their lives. The way law stays alive is by remaining in touch with social contracts pieced together among real people on the ground.

The Parallel with US History

It is hard to grasp just how important extralegal pressure and political responsiveness were in the United States by reading indiscriminately through the US history section of a library. Nor will it be easy for most reform-minded politicians and technocrats to discover the American history they should most care about, namely, the connection between the legalization of property and the creation of capital. To be socially and politically useful, history has to be assembled to illuminate the problem at hand. And, by and large, property specialists have not written about the transition from extralegal rights to an integrated legal property system. There may be several reasons for this.

First, the historical process is not yet complete. Contrary to popular belief, property systems open to all citizens are a relatively recent phenomenon – no more than two hundred years old – and the full implications of the transition have yet to emerge. In most nations of the West the major task of widespread property reform was completed only about a century ago; in Japan it has been in place for less than fifty years. Since the whole process that created integrated property systems was more the result of unconscious evolution than conscious planning, it is not surprising that it may require time for all the useful lessons of property creation in advanced nations to become apparent to people in the developing world.

Second, property has traditionally been considered from the point of view of the advanced nations. Most of today's burgeoning literature on property takes its genesis in the West for granted.

The third reason why the process of formal property creation is difficult to grasp is that it is hard to follow the thread of the story. The slow absorption of the practices, customs and norms of extralegals into formal law has been obscured by other historical events. The granting of formal property rights to settlers and squatters in the United States, which eventually created the basis for capital generation and transactions in an expanded market, is typically treated as a political strategy to aid American imperial ambitions, help pioneers exploit the country's vast resources, and ease sectional tensions. That these same steps may have also permitted the United States to transcend the conflict between the legal system and the extralegal arrangements of squatters and other pioneers has not been the primary focus of property specialists.

What I intend in this chapter, let me emphasize again, is not to rewrite the history of the United States, but to rearrange the familiar narrative in a way that will help us understand that the apparent chaos in developing and former communist nations is actually a search for a new legal order. Let us look, then, at the transition of extralegal 'law' from the woods and fields of the infant United States into its law books.

Leaving behind Antiquated British Law

The sixteenth century saw the beginning of an unprecedented migration of Western Europeans to the shores of North and South America —what the historian Bernard Bailyn has called 'one of the greatest events in recorded history'.[2] In British North America, according to Hoffer, a 'cold, tired, apprehensive assemblage of men and women . . . gathered on the western shore of the Atlantic, peering into a densely wooded wilderness. Clutching blunderbusses and Bibles, some must have summoned memories of the world they had left behind.'[3]

Among those memories were notions of how to build and maintain communities, settle disputes, acquire land and construct government institutions. The legal system played a prominent role in resolving the conflicts these actions invariably created. Indeed, the law 'went everywhere' in early America as 'the first colonial governments were based on legal documents – "charters" . . . Colonial economies functioned under laws regulating prices, wages, and the quality of articles. Law gave the means for people to sell or will their land to others, provided a forum for settling arguments about broken fences and straying livestock, and even told people how to worship, marry, rear their children and treat their servants and neighbors.'[4]

Initially colonists attempted to apply the doctrines of English property law to bring order. But English common law had not envisioned a society that was rapidly generating new forms of property access without an established and generally accepted titling system. English common law, for example, did not provide guidance for how courts should handle cases involving people who had bought or inherited land of dubious title. As a result, 'open trials of title in the county courts became absolutely necessary. All interested parties were able to testify, and the court's decision stood as a relatively effective and public guarantee where none other existed.'[5]

Most of these colonists, however, had little comprehension

of the technicalities of English law. Many did not know or care to know the differences between legal writs, law and equity, and other subtleties. More importantly, the English common law of property was often ill-suited to deal with the problems that confronted the colonists. A superabundance of land in British North America presented the first settlers with opportunities unimaginable in the Europe they had left. Arriving 'on a continent where much land was naturally clear or had been cleared by Indians, Englishmen [and other Europeans] rushed to apportion their new source of wealth ... As a result, scrupulous regard to detail was easily overlooked. Inexactness in allotment and recording was tolerated, and little attention was given to the orderly plans which, it had been expected [by colonial authorities,] were to be followed.'[6] Not all of the land was fertile, well drained, or within easy reach of meadows to supply hay for the settlers' cattle and horses.[7] In their search for suitable land American colonists often moved at whim, laying out boundaries, cultivating fields, building houses – and then abandoning it all to move on to more fertile territory.

The result for property rights was a great deal of variability and extralegality. In his analysis of legal change in colonial Massachusetts, David Thomas Konig provides an outline of the bureaucratic and technical failures that exacerbated the problems of migration. The lack of a uniform surveying system, for example, created divergences and irregularities. Throughout Massachusetts, colonial authorities often disagreed over how lands should be divided. There 'was not agreement, for example, as to whether straight lines or natural features should be used to separate land holdings'. One colonist 'had assumed that his grant of three hundred acres in Reading was rectangular in shape, but to his dismay he later discovered that the lot of his neighbor in the next town had been laid out in a "circular form" whose arc subtracted from [the colonist's] acreage'.[8] Technical shortcomings in the surveying procedures also added to the uncertainty and confusion. Konig notes that difficulties in compensating for the variation of the meridian in North America often created over-lapping property claims, until John Winthrop IV produced a table of variations for land surveying in 1763.[9]

In crafting decisions for a bewildering array of property disputes, the nature of which had few or no English precedents, colonial authorities could not easily defer to English jurisprudence. Instead, 'the courts often turned to local town customs and transformed them into a new body of law that would stabilize land dealings'.[10] In matters ranging from domestic political autonomy to the use and distribution of land, colonists began to deviate in significant ways from English laws that had little or no logical relevance to the realities of colonial life. As Peter Charles Hoffer emphasizes: 'In theory they were part of the king's personal domain [and subject to all his laws], but fact preempted theory. Far from England, thinly populated, rich in natural resources, and occupied by men and women who knew their own minds and grasped a bargain when they saw it, the colonies edged towards self-government.'[11]

An Early American Tradition – Squatting

Although early migrants were mainly British subjects and obeyed English law, once they moved to America, a different reality, the way they related to each other began to change. In England occupying a plot of land for a long period without a title – 'squatting' – was against the law. In the United States, with no initial resistance and many opportunities, squatting on available land quickly became a common practice. Squatting is older than the nation itself. According to Amelia Ford's study of the colonial precedents of the US land system, 'before the arrival of the Massachusetts Bay Company in New England, there were settlers without charter or grant living at various places within the limits of the Bay . . . the first Connecticut settlers were legally trespassers on their territory, and could base their rights only in occupation and purchase from the Indians'.[12] During Maryland's early years Frenchmen and other non-English people resided on land that they were incapable of owning under the conditions of the grant. And in 1727 Pennsylvania legislators protested those 'sorts [who] sitt frequently down on any spott of vacant Land they can find'. These colonial American squatters had already occupied and improved 100,000 acres of land without, as one historian put it, a 'shadow of a right'.[13]

In New England propertied politicians found no virtue in the activities of squatters whom they regarded simply as illegal trespassers. As early as 1634 in Massachusetts the General Court attempted to restrict squatting by ordering 'that all land grants to freemen be recorded and a transcript be sent to it. Surveying was to be done in each town by a constable and four other freemen.'[14] This did not work either. The widespread failure of those who occupied land 'to follow the injunctions of 1634 and 1635 forced the General Court [in 1637] to act once more and demand "that some course bee taken to cause men to record their lands, or to fine them that neglect" '.[15]

However, there were no effective legal means to reconcile many of the conflicts that arose. As a result, squatters turned to *de facto* devices that created openings for legitimizing squatting. Many of the most intense conflicts took place on the largely vacant outlying territories now known as Vermont and Maine. Prior to the American Revolution, both New York and New Hampshire claimed the territory of Vermont.[16] In order to circumvent New York's claim Governor Benning Wentworth of New Hampshire, 'acting on the principle that possession was nine tenths of the law . . . made free grants in the region to both New Hampshire and Massachusetts citizens . . . [The result was that between 1764 and 1769] 131 townships were granted to more than six thousand . . . select groups of individuals.'[17]

Following closely on their heels, squatters with little allegiance to any state soon overran the territory. Indeed, 'settlers began streaming into Vermont and settling wherever it suited their fancy'.[18] Early on they realized the importance of collective action and began 'to petition first New Hampshire and later the Governor of New York for a grant of land to include their settlements, or an ordinance confirming them in their lands'.[19] Although both colonies attempted to thwart the squatters' claims by repeatedly bringing ejectment proceedings against them, squatter dominance of the territory was so complete that Ethan Allen and his 'squatter followers' won statehood for Vermont following the Revolution. A primary result of this extraordinary triumph of 'squatter power' was formal recognition of their property arrangements.

Squatting was often fuelled by propertied politicians eager to develop and exploit a colony's resources. In most colonies politicians believed that territorial development could be accomplished only through immigration. To accomplish this goal, colonial politicians gave grants to individuals and groups to settle on undeveloped land, predicating the passage of title on occupation and improvement. In Virginia, according to Ford, 'to seat the tract meant to build a house, plant one acre, and keep stock for one year; if this were not done within three years, the land lapsed to the state'.[20] Under Massachusetts law, a settler's duties 'included taking actual possession and within three years, building a house of a certain size, usually eighteen or twenty feet square, and clearing five to eight acres for mowing and tilling'.[21]

In Maryland during the 1670s Lord Baltimore used squatters to 'settle some disputed territory on the seaboard side on the Eastern Shore and on Delaware Bay'.[22] In a measure to keep their own revenue stream from being broken, the Penns in Pennsylvania 'sent directions that people who had settled on any lands could have them at the price in vogue at the time of settlement with interest from that time but minus the value of improvements; those who could not do this were obliged to pay a quitrent proportioned to the purchase money'.[23] As the Penns soon discovered, however, such a directive proved exceedingly difficult to enforce if squatters did not want to pay. In fact, 'it became clear that unless some modus vivendi was established with these determined, land hungry men, who could not be driven away, large revenues would inevitably be lost . . . Accordingly, [Pennsylvania's] land office connived at or permitted many usages it was powerless to prevent and there arose besides the regular office rights, many particular, local species of land titles.'[24]

In securing the rights they hoped to achieve through such settlement policies, squatters often found the formal system too burdensome or complex. As Amelia Ford also notes, 'the land office was too distant, affairs too confused, and methods too dilatory to suit the practical' squatters.[25] British laws were becoming increasingly irrelevant to the way many people lived and worked.

The New Social Contract: 'Tomahawk Rights'

In the chaos surrounding law, land and property the migrants realized that if they were going to live in peace among themselves, they had to establish some sort of order, even if it had to be outside the official law. Squatters began inventing their own species of extralegal property titles known as 'tomahawk rights', 'cabin rights' and 'corn rights'. 'Tomahawk rights' were secured by deadening a few trees near the head of a spring and marking the bark of one or more trees with the initials of the person who made the improvement. As early as the 1660s squatters in Maryland developed the custom of marking trees on the lands they wanted before they were surveyed with the permission of the colony's 'surveyor-general'.[26] By the end of the American Revolution the practice of marking trees for possessory right to lands had become so prominent that one army official wrote to the Secretary of War: 'These men on the frontier have been accustomed to seat themselves on the best of the lands, making a tomahawk right or improvement, as they term it, supposing that to be a suffi-cient title.'[27]

'Cabin rights' and 'corn rights' meant staking out land by building a log cabin or raising a crop of corn. Significantly, these extralegal rights were bought, sold and transferred – just like official titles.[28] And while such cabin or corn rights may not have legally entitled anyone to the land, there is no question that such extralegal property rights helped avoid quarrels, were widely accepted in America's frontier com-munities, and became the source of legal title years later.

Despite the implicit acquiescence of local politicians to these extralegal arrangements, squatters still encountered a hostile world. They were constantly provoking conflict with Native Americans by invading their lands. But squatters were also a threat to the élite, who feared losing their vast properties. That is why one member of the élite – George Washington – complained in 1783 of the 'Banditti who will bidd defiance to all Authority while they are skimming and disposing of the Cream of the Country at the expense of many.'[29]

Shooting the Sheriff

Migrants began settling boundaries, ploughing fields, building homes, transferring land and establishing credit long before governments had conferred on them the right to do so. Despite their enterprise, however, many authorities remained con-vinced that these new Americans were flagrantly disobeying the law and should be prosecuted. But this was not easy to do. Even when George Washington, the father of the United States, tried to eject the people who had squatted on his Virginia farmland, his lawyer warned that 'if he succeeded in his suit against the settlers on his estate, they would probably burn his barns and fences'.[30]

Relations between other states and local squatters also began to heat up. Even before the Revolution migrants from

Massachusetts had already begun to settle in Maine, a territory that Massachusetts claimed as early as 1691. At first, Massachusetts politicians tolerated the rapid increase in squatters in distant Maine. After the Revolution, however, with its treasury bankrupt and its currency depreciated, Massachusetts politicians looked upon the vast lands of Maine as a major source of new revenue.[31] Suddenly, the Maine squatters were an obstacle to the sale of large blocks of land. In 1786 the governor issued a proclamation prohibiting squatting in Maine.[32]

To reassure potential purchasers Massachusetts appointed a committee to investigate and demand payment from illegal 'trespassers'.[33] Most squatters, however, simply refused to move or pay for their lands. Rather than compromise with the squatters, the state ordered sheriffs to enforce legal ejectment procedures, igniting a powder-keg that led to what one historian described as 'something like open warfare'.

'The most prominent feature in [the squatter's] character is a violent and implacable hatred to the law,' commented one Maine lawyer in 1800. 'The sheriff of the county and his officers they have marked out doomed as victims for sacrifice and the hated name of execution [of writs in ejectment proceedings] is to terrify them no more. They declare the profession of law must come down, that lawyers must be extirpated and their offices prostrated with the dust.'[34] And when a sheriff was killed while trying to oust a squatter, juries refused to convict the alleged murderer. Partly as a result of the political ramifications of the hostility among the Maine squatters, Massachusetts consented to the statehood of Maine in 1820.[35]

Other colonies also did their best to suppress squatting on public and private lands. In Pennsylvania Scots–Irish settlers began moving into Indian lands as early as 1730, and the Native Americans fought back. Colonial authorities repeatedly warned the settlers 'against stealing the Indian's land, and by way of instruction burned their cabins'.[36] Indeed, from 1763 to

1768 the Pennsylvania Assembly tried to deter squatting with the penalty of 'pain of death', while Governor William Penn ordered soldiers to remove illegal settlers.[37] Despite these measures, the number of squatters doubled. In response, according to one historian of the period, 'the infuriated governor then proclaimed that those settling on Indian lands would be executed. But no judges could be found for such prisoners, or compliant juries and secure lockups.'[38]

The Legal Breakthrough: 'Pre-emption'

In a country where every settler was either a migrant or related to one, the squatters were bound to have supporters among colonial authorities who realized how difficult it would be to apply English common law to many new settlers. Under English law, even if someone mistakenly squatted on another person's land and made improvements, he could not recover the value of what he had done. In the colonies, however, given the lack of effective government and reliable records and surveys, authorities had to accept that improvements made on land, taxes paid and local arrangements among neighbours were also acceptable sources of property rights. As early as 1642 the colony of Virginia allowed a wrongful possessor to recover the value of any improvements from the true owner. The Virginia statute noted that 'if any person or persons whatsoever have sett downe upon any plantation or ground which did properly belong to any other man [a] valuable consideration [is to] be allowed by the judgment of twelve men'.[39] Moreover, if the rightful owner was unwilling to reimburse the squatter for these improvements, the squatter could purchase the land at a price set by a local jury.[40] This statute was soon copied by other colonies. Such clauses demonstrated the extent to which local élites were sympathetic to people who wanted to generate surplus value from their land.

This legal innovation of allowing a settler to buy the land he had improved before it was offered for public sale was known as 'pre-emption' – a principle that would be the key to the integration of extralegal property arrangements in American law over the next two hundred years. Politicians and jurists began to interpret 'improvement' in ways that heavily benefited squatters. In North Carolina and Virginia cabin rights or corn rights counted as improvements.[41] In Massachusetts tomahawk rights were included.[42] Significantly, incorporating such local extralegal arrangements into the law 'was not only a recognition that some allowance was due first settlers for the charge and risk they had incurred; it was a legal expression of a wide-spread sentiment .. . .. that the squatter was really a benefactor to the state, and not a trespasser'.[43] By the time of the American Revolution the 'corn rights' of the itinerant squatter had been transformed, in many people's minds, into the occupancy rights of the hardy pioneer. Even as George Washington was lamenting the 'banditti' who had invaded his own land, elsewhere in his home state of Virginia other politicians were encouraging squatters by protecting their extralegal titles.

For states with little money, pre-emption was also a source of revenue. They would charge squatters for surveying the land they had improved and for issuing legal title. As a result, pre-emption laws proliferated both before and after the Revolution. In 1777 North Carolina opened up a landed office for a western county, permitting settlers to take 640 acres, giving preference to people already squatting in the area.[44] Two years later Virginia passed a law that gave settlers who had squatted on its western borders the right to pre-emption on land that they had improved.[45]

More Legal Obstacles – More Extralegals

Having won many battles, the American squatters, however, were far from winning the war. The ambivalence towards extralegals persisted during the United States' first century, and nowhere was it more evident than in the new federal government, suddenly in control of vast public lands. From about 1784 to 1850, the United States acquired almost 900 million acres through conquest and purchase: the Louisiana Purchase (1803) included 500 million acres; the Florida Purchase (1819) 43 million acres; the Gadsen Purchase (1853) 19 million acres; war with Mexico (1848) won 334 million acres.[46] In addition, by 1802 the federal government had acquired all the western territories of the eastern seaboard states.

Beginning in 1784, the Congress of the newly confederated (though not yet constitutionally united) states began formulating plans to restrict access and rights to the national domain. The most momentous decision was that settlements in the Northwest Territory would ultimately become states with the same rights and privileges as the original thirteen.[47] In 1785 Congress expanded the previous year's ordinance by providing a system of surveying and selling the public lands. Following the model used in the New England colonies, the surveying system divided land into townships six miles square with the townships further subdivided into thirty-six sections of one square mile or 640 acres. Once the area had been surveyed, these 640-acre sections were to be sold at one dollar an acre.

In 1787 Congress consolidated the previous ordinances into the Northwest Ordinance, which provided for the division of the Northwest Territory into several sections, and laid out three stages of increasing representation that would lead to statehood. Notably, the law established the concept of 'fee simple ownership' (estates were held in perpetuity with unlimited power to sell or give them away) and provided the first guarantee of freedom of contract in the United States.[48] Although such federal laws provided an elegant structure of formal law for the distribution of public lands – historians view the Northwest Ordinance as the prime achievement of the pre-Constitution US government – they could neither control nor contain the increasing number of people migrating to the nation's periphery. One major problem was the prohibitive price of federal land. Faced with a price tag of $640 – a huge sum at the time – thousands of America's migrants were immediately priced out of the federal land market.[49] The drafters of the Northwest Ordinances, however, assumed wealthy investors would sell off the tracts in smaller parcels, extend credit, or make favourable leases to the land. Even these speculative options were often beyond the means of the pioneer.[50] Migrants instead 'chose the uncertainties of unlawful settlement'.[51] And thus tens of thousands more Americans became squatters on the basis of extralegal arrangements.

Almost immediately the federal government worked to marginalize and penalize these squatters. They were ardently attacked in the debates surrounding the adoption of the Northwest Ordinance. William Butler of New York wrote: 'I Presume Council has been made acquainted with the villainy of the People of this Country, that are flocking from all Quarters, settling & taking up not only the United States lands but also this States, many Hundreds have crossed the Rivers, & are dayly going many with their family's, the Wisdom of Council I hope will Provide against so gross and growing an evil.'[52] Heavily influenced by such sentiment, members of Congress worked to dislodge squatters, often by violent means. In 1785 Congress passed a resolution explicitly prohibiting squatting in the public domain and giving the Secretary of War authority to remove unlawful settlers from federal lands in the Northwest Territory. This policy went into effect in the spring of 1785 at the juncture of the Muskingum and Ohio rivers where the US Army dispossessed ten families by destroying their homes while constructing a fort to prevent them from returning.[53] Four years later President Washington ordered the destruction of cabins and the removal of families who settled on Pennsylvania frontier land owned by Native Americans.[54]

However, though most politicians wanted to uphold the

established law of the new sovereign nation, some already doubted that it could be enforced in such a way that it would suit the best interests of the country. That is why the question of pre-emption came up almost at once.[55] During the very first session of the new Congress, in 1789, one member poignantly outlined the choices that squatters faced:

> There are, at this moment, a great number of people on the ground, who are willing to acquire by purchase a right to the soil they are seated upon. What will these men think, who have placed themselves on the vacant spot, anxiously waiting its disposition by the Government, to find their preemption right engrossed by the purchase of a million acres? Will they expect themselves to be preyed upon by these men? . . . They will do one of two things: either move into the Spanish territory, where they are not altogether uninvited, and become an accession of power to a foreign nation forming to us a dangerous frontier; or they will take this course, move on the United States territory, and take possession without your leave. What then will be the case? They will not pay you money. Will you then raise a force to drive them off? That has been tried; troops were raised, and sent . . . to effect that purpose. They burnt the cabins, broke down the fences, and tore up the potatoe patches; but three hours after the troops were gone, these people returned again, repaired the damage, and are now settled upon the land in open defiance of the Union.[56]

Typical of the ambivalence in Congress at the time were the views of the Public Lands Committee of the House of Representatives. Recommending in 1801 that Congress refuse requests by squatters for pre-emptive rights, the committee acknowledged that the squatters had, 'with much labor and difficulty, settled upon, cultivated, and improved certain lands . . . [and thereby] not only enhanced the value of the lands respectively settled, but of the land in the vicinity of the same, to the great benefit of the United States'. Regardless, the committee argued that to grant 'the indulgence prayed for would operate as an encouragement to intrusions on public lands, and would be an unjustifiable sacrifice of the public interest'.[57] And so the prevailing sentiment among Congressmen was to deny them any rights.

In the two decades following its institution according to Article One of the US Constitution, Congress steadfastly held to its antagonism towards settlers residing illegally on the public domain. In 1796 it raised the minimum price for public lands from the $1 per acre set in the Land Ordinance of 1785 to $2 per acre.[58] In 1807 Congress passed a measure that provided for fines and imprisonment for any squatter who failed to comply with the law once notified and authorized force to remove illegal settlers if necessary.[59] An 1812 document of the House Committee on Public Lands noted: 'Promiscuous and unauthorized settlement on public lands are in many respects, injurious to the public interest.'[60]

The problem, however, was that Congress, as is the case in many countries today, was out of touch with reality: it had no conception of the sheer dimension of the pressure from squatters, nor did it have the means to impose its mandates. Even the General Land Office, established in 1812 to survey, sell and register the public lands, could not do its job. Charged with confirming land patents sent in from the district offices, the new federal agency also had to oversee the record-keeping of purchases made on credit. Lawmakers hoped that the Land Office would operate as an information centre serving citizens requiring land. But all these tasks soon overwhelmed its small staff, which quickly fell behind in most of their duties.[61] As Patricia Nelson Limerick points out, Congressmen themselves contributed to the Land Office's problems: 'On behalf of their constituents, congressmen complained of the slowness with which the office worked; on their own behalf, congressmen made many of the requests for information that ate up the clerks' time; and for the sake of economy and retrenchment, congressmen refused to increase the office's appropriations.'[62]

In addition, in the early days the United States possessed limited financial resources and had to resort to land grants to compensate certain sectors of the population. Various historians feel that by the practice of issuing 'land scrip', which has been described as 'the nineteenth-century equivalent of food stamps' – paper that was redeemable in land – the government encouraged lawlessness and squatting.[63] From 1780 to 1848 Congress provided 2 million acres of land for the soldiers who fought in the Revolution, 5 million to veterans of the war of 1812, and 13 million for those who fought in the war with Mexico. Between 1851 and 1860 Congress added another 44 million acres for service in the Revolutionary War, the war of 1812, the Indian Wars and the Mexican–American War.[64] When first conceived by the Continental Congress during the War for Independence, the land scrip policy had a certain logic in that it allowed the American government to pay officers and soldiers for their service. Congress also feared the continuing military threat that indigenous populations, either on their own or as paid mercenaries of the English or French, posed for the new republic. The aim of settling former soldiers on the frontier was to solve both problems at once.

By the middle of the nineteenth century, however, a thriving black market in land scrip emerged that fuelled both squatting and speculation. For every hundred soldiers who received land scrip, eighty-four sold their rights in the black market – a situation similar to the one that occurs today in many developing and former communist countries which have provided public housing for some groups of citizens.[65] As one historian puts it, 'no one expected the half million widows and elderly men who received [scrip] to form a barrier against foreign invasion'.[66]

The federal government also gave millions of acres of free land to the new railroad crisscrossing the continent. During the nineteenth century, over 318 million acres – almost one-fifth of all federal lands – were handed out, either directly to private railroad companies or to states who would then redistribute the land to the railroads. The rationale for this massive giveaway was that it would promote orderly settlement of the frontier. Although much of the land was of little value, a sizeable portion did contain minerals or was arable.[67] The lion's share went to the transcontinental railroads who received only every other section of land along their routes, creating a checkerboard pattern of alternating government and railroad land. Congress believed that the railroads would sell the land they didn't need quickly and cheaply to encourage settlement.[68] Yet, once again, the realities of land settlement conflicted with the hopes of politicians. The checkerboard arrangement, according to one scholar, 'delayed settlement on millions of acres of the best lands and had closed them to acquisition'.[69] In certain cases it even led to open warfare between the railroad companies and settlers. Stephen Schwartz reports on the conflict that arose in 1880, in the San Joaquin Valley of California, then called Mussel Slough, when farmers and ranchers establishing themselves on railroad properties could not come to a sales agreement with the railroad companies. This led not only to court action that could not resolve the case, but to shooting causing the deaths of five settlers in which the responsible marshal admitted that he was 'not certain who fired first'. Editorializing on the incident, the *San Francisco Chronicle* condemned the railroads, stating that 'Whatever might be their strictly legal rights, it is undeniable that all the equities were in favor of the settlers.' In any case physical force was also on the side of the settlers, since officials estimated that to dislodge them somewhere between 200 and 1,000 good soldiers would be required.[70]

The federal government's efforts to construct an orderly land system could not overcome the will of the common people to assert their right to the national domain. One articulate squatter argued: 'I do certify that all mankind agreeable to every constitution formed in America, have an undoubted right to pass into every vacant country and . . . Congress is not empowered to forbid them.'[71] During the first several decades of the nineteenth century, politicians and squatters battled over how property rights would be conveyed. Among politicians, 'the question arose: "What is to be done with it?" "Give it to the soldiers," demanded some. "Use it to pay off the national debt," said others. "Keep it for future use," still others counseled, and there were those who held that any who desired should have the right to settle on it.'[72]

Lawlessness or Clash of Legal Systems?

At the beginning of the nineteenth century the property system of the United States was in a state of disarray. Existing property law and antagonistic legislators only exacerbated the crisis facing the nation's migrants. In his seminal study of squatters and land laws in Virginia and Kentucky Paul Gates argues that the formal law contributed to 'ever growing costs of litigation to clear titles, eject persons with rival claims, and protect land from intrusion and plunder'. Combined 'with court fees and the high interest on borrowed capital', the inadequacy of formal law was a 'constant threat to the security of investments and kept litigants in continued turmoil'.[73]

Predictably, the migrants who settled these lands, more often than not, did not have formal title to their property and usually ended up having to negotiate for the title with not one but two owners; and then even after they had purchased the land and made their improvements, they were likely to be faced with ejectment proceedings brought by others with prior rights to their tracts.[74] One foreign visitor travelling through Kentucky in 1802 noted that at every house he stopped in, the owner expressed doubt about the soundness of his neighbours' titles.[75]

Between 1785 and 1890 the United States Congress passed over five hundred different laws to reform the property system, ostensibly based on the Jeffersonian ideal of putting property into the hands of private citizens. The complicated procedures associated with these laws, however, often hampered this goal. To confuse matters further, individual states developed their own rules of property and land distribution that largely benefited and protected only their own propertied élite. As a result, attempts to reform the property system only served to heighten the nation's land difficulties while making migrants extremely wary about losing what semblance of title they may have possessed. Commenting on reform in Kentucky, one contemporary emphasized that 'many of the inhabitants derive the security of their estates from this confusion ... [and consequently] many dare not assert their rights, from a fear of being obliged to pay considerable indemnifications'.[76] During the eighteenth century and the early nineteenth, 'as old problems were solved, new ones emerged. There were chronic difficulties in determining title ... [as title became a] concept more elusive than longitude, more nebulous than a tree stump or stream. Title became as vexatious and intractable a subject as the abolished law of tenure.'[77] Quite simply, the legal institutions of the United States failed, in fundamental ways, to deal effectively with the burgeoning migrant population.

By 1820 the original US property system was in such disarray that Supreme Court Justice Joseph Story wrote: 'Ages will probably lapse before litigations founded on [the US property laws] will be closed ... It will forever remain an unknown code, with a peculiar dialect, to be explored and studied, like the jurisprudence of some foreign nation.'[78] The irony was not lost on Justice Story that the United States was 'not an old conservative society but a new state at the legal periphery'.[79]

US laws had become so cumbersome that they constituted a major stumbling block for settlers who wanted to secure their property rights and thus break out of their status as 'squatters'. They were left no alternative but to begin fashioning their own 'laws', especially those pertaining to property, fusing English law and the home grown American legal traditions with their own common sense. The result was 'a phalanx of vested property rights'[80] in two legal and economic systems, one sitting codified and in the statute books, the other operating on the ground. And thus the United States found itself with a pluralistic legal system in which many rights over property and ownership arrangements came to be defined by extralegal law.

The political and legal establishments were caught between their allegiance to formal law and their sympathy towards the settlers' need to create their own arrangements. A speech by Thomas Jefferson captures perfectly the ambivalence politicians have always felt towards the extralegal arrangements in their midst. 'So multifarious were [these arrangements] ... that no established principles of law or equity could be applied for their determination; many of them being built on customs and habits which had grown up in that County, being founded on modes of transmission peculiar to themselves, and which, having entered into almost every title *could not be absolutely neglected.*'[81]

State Efforts to Lift the Bell Jar

American politicians thus had several choices. They could continue to try to thwart or ignore extralegals, grudgingly make concessions or become champions of extralegal rights. The expansion of occupancy laws – recognizing a right to land based on improvements made on it – throughout the United States during the first sixty years of the nineteenth century suggests that politicians increasingly followed the last course. The history of the adoption of occupancy laws in the United States is the history of the rise of extralegals as a political force.

The turning point came in the new state of Kentucky, whose property system, like that of many states, was in complete disarray. Its governor complained that land claims in the new state added up to three times its area. Paul Gates argues that this was due to politicians' passing legislation that catered to extralegal constituencies between 1797 and 1820. These measures contributed to 'the two great principles of equity in [American] statutory law: The right of occupants. . . to their improvements and the right of settlers on privately owned land, unchallenged for seven years and paying taxes thereon, to a firm and clear title to their land no matter what adverse titles might be outstanding.'[82] The importance of the Kentucky legislation, however, lay not in its contribution to legal doctrine but in its reflection of the growing political power of the pioneers. Significantly, the pressure these extralegal settlers exerted on elected officials would lead many state governments to reject a US Supreme Court decision antagonistic to the nation's large extralegal population.

In 1821 the Court declared Kentucky's occupancy law unconstitutional.[83] The case involved the heirs of large landowner John Green and Richard Biddle, a squatter who had settled upon Green's land illegally. The disputed land had originally been in Virginia but was now part of Kentucky. In *Green v. Biddle* the Supreme Court ruled against Kentucky's occupancy law by pointing to 'rules of property' established under the precedents of English common law.[84]

The decision explicitly favoured only those people who held legal title to the land they occupied. According to the Court, the Kentucky law 'operated unjustly and oppressively because the lawful owner is compelled to pay, not merely for the actual ameliorations in the land, not its increased value only, but the expense incurred by the occupant in making pretended improvements, whether they are merely useful or fanciful, and matter of taste or ornaments only dictated by his whim and caprice'.[85] After rehearing *Green v. Biddle*, the Court, in 1823, reaffirmed its previous decision, emphasizing that the occupancy laws deprived 'the rightful owner of the land, of the rents and profits received by the occupants'.

Politicians who had been cultivating the support of their extralegal constituents lambasted *Biddle* as 'most ruinous' and causing 'great alarm' for Kentuckians.[86] The Supreme Court might be oblivious to the new political – and legal – reality taking shape in the rapidly expanding American frontier, but Western politicians only had to look out of their windows to see how quickly the country was changing. In the early decades of the nineteenth century, tens of thousands of hardy migrants had trudged westward from the original colonies over the Appalachian Mountains to settle on fertile, virgin lands. The US population had been doubling every twenty years. In 1620 there had been approximately five thousand settlers in all of British North America. In 1860 the US population would be more than 30 million and counting. Fifty per cent of the American population lived west of the Appalachians.

These migrants wanted the courts to recognize their rights to the property they had acquired.[87] Thus the political and judicial backlash to the Supreme Court's decision in *Green v. Biddle* in Kentucky was a huge victory for the extralegals, and they quickly went on the offensive. In the minds of many politicians and the local newspaper editors the villain was now the US Supreme Court. One local paper spoke of the 'treacherous conduct' of justices who threatened to 'exterminate' the rights of 'nonresidents and aliens'.[88] In the midst of the furor over the Court's authority, Kentucky's powerful Richard M. Johnson declared in a speech before the Senate that the decision 'would overturn the deliberate policy of [Kentucky] . . . and, if persisted in, would produce the most disastrous consequences in giving rise to much litigation where questions had been settled for years, and put everything respecting landed property into the greatest confusion'.[89] Kentucky's other and even more influential US senator, Henry Clay, long an opponent of liberally extending squatter rights, conceded: 'They build houses, plant orchards, enclose fields, cultivate the earth, and rear up families around them. Meantime, the tide of emigration flows upon them, their improved farms rise in value, a demand for them takes place, they sell to the newcomers at a great advance, and proceed farther west . . . In this way, thousands and tens of thousands are daily improving their circumstances and bettering their conditions.'[90] Both the governor and the Kentucky legislature also voiced their opposition to the Supreme Court's decision.[91]

Since its inception, the Court had been a prime target of politicians critical of the authority of an élite group of judges elected by no one. But, in an extraordinary turn of events, Kentucky judges also rejected the Supreme Court's decision. In a similar case two years later a Kentucky judge noted that *Green v. Biddle* could not be followed because the case 'was decided by three only of the seven judges that composed the Supreme Court of the United States; and being the opinion of less than a majority of the judges cannot be considered as having settled a constitutional principle'.[92] In 1827 another Kentucky judge rejected *Biddle*, emphasizing that the occupying claimants law was constitutional in 'cases too numerous to be quoted'.[93]

In the wake of the furor over *Green v. Biddle* Western politicians and Democrats from around the country began viewing this growing constituency of squatters through a different prism. No longer were they scruffy criminals skimming the cream of the nation's lands but 'noble pioneers' helping to develop the country. Of course, they were also potential voters.[94] Sympathetic politicians began attacking the property system. One Congressman from Kansas emphasized, 'all over [this] state settlers had taken up public lands, made their improvements, paid their fees, and were later ordered off the land without redress by decisions of the Secretary of Interior, for one reason or another'.[95]

Federal Efforts to Lift the Bell Jar

In the middle of the dispute over *Green v. Biddle* Andrew Jackson, a hero of the war of 1812 against the British and a vocal supporter of the pioneers, almost won the presidency. Four years later Jackson finally did become president. During his two-term administration, as the last property qualifications for voting and running for political office disappeared, as public schools proliferated, as the states humanized penal codes and closed down debtor prisons, sympathy for the rights of squatters increased. So did public animosity towards judges and attorneys, who were perceived as eager agents of the rich and the powerful.[96]

By 1830 the thirteen original states were twenty-four, including seven in the West whose representatives in Washington were fully committed to policies that favoured the squatters. To gain the support of this increasingly influential bloc, Northern and Southern states competed to show how pro-Western they were.[97] The Western states and the squatters who dominated the land there started to flex their growing political muscles, and the results were impressive. Between 1834 and 1856 Missouri, Alabama, Arkansas, Michigan, Iowa, Mississippi, Wisconsin, Minnesota, Oregon, Kansas and California all adopted occupancy laws similar to the Kentucky law rejected by the Supreme Court in *Green v. Biddle*.[98] Paul Gates argues that 'no case decided by the Supreme Court had been so completely overturned by state legislation and state courts, by failure of the federal courts to make use of the case, and finally by the unchallenged act of Congress extending the coverage of federal courts to occupants as *Green v. Biddle*'.[99]

Washington finally began to get the message. While in 1806 the Public Lands Committee had blamed squatters for their own hardships, by 1828 the same committee was reporting to the House of Representatives that the American squatter had performed a valuable public service for which he deserved compensation.[100] The once dreaded squatter was now some-one 'who by his enterprise and industry has created for himself and his family a home in the wilderness, should be entitled to his reward. He has afforded facilities to the sale of public lands, and brought into competition lands which otherwise would have commanded no price and for which there would have been no bidders, unless for his improvements.'[101]

Members of Congress began drafting legislation that helped ease the way for settlers' arrangements to be absorbed into the legal system.[102] At its centre was the legal device that had been the squatter's salvation during the colonial period (and that the US Congress had adamantly opposed) – pre-emption. In 1830 a coalition of Western and Southern Congressmen passed a general pre-emption act that applied 'to every settler or occupant of the public lands . . . who is now in possession, and cultivated any part thereof in the year one thousand eight hundred and twenty-nine'.[103] A squatter could claim 160 acres of land, including lands he had improved, for $1.25 per acre. Payment was required before the land was set for public auction, and transfers or sales of pre-emptive rights were strictly forbidden.

In 1832, 1838 and 1840 Congress renewed the general pre-emption act of 1830. Each time it attempted to strengthen further the rights of the lowest squatter, while trying to block some of the abuses of the pre-emption principle. For instance, the 1832 act lowered the minimum amount of land a squatter had to purchase from 160 to 40 acres.

By 1841 the pre-emption principle had become so firmly established that Congress enacted a general prospective pre-emption bill. The 1841 act covered not only existing squatters but 'every person . . . who shall hereafter make a settlement on the public lands'.[104] The settled land had to be surveyed, but even this provision was eventually overturned.[105]

Extralegal Efforts to Lift the Bell Jar

Often geographically isolated from the political and constitutional debates over property, many squatters did everything they could to secure the land they occupied; some even paid twice for the same parcel, while others paid lawyers enormous fees to help them make their land legal.[106] Many did not have the means to cover the costs of the official legal system, so they established their own extralegal arrangements, thus creating new avenues for accessing and holding property on the American frontier. For all practical purposes, they took the law into their own hands – and forced the legal establishment to follow their lead. It took the politicians some time before they awakened to the fact that, alongside the official law, extralegal social contracts for property had taken shape and that they constituted an essential part of the nation's property rights system; that to establish a comprehensive legal system that could be enforced throughout the nation they would have to catch up with the way people were defining, using and distributing property rights.

Two important examples serve to illustrate the emergence of extralegal organizations to protect informally acquired property rights: the claim associations that proliferated throughout the American Midwest during the first half of the nineteenth century, and the miner districts that saturated the American West after the discovery of gold in California. For many American historians, claim associations and miner regulations represented the 'manifestation of the frontier man's capacity for democratic action',[107] Others have argued that these organizations operated 'as a smoke screen to obscure the theft of land from bona fide owners'.[108] That is not my debate. What interests me about the claim associations and miner organizations is that they show that extralegal groups played an important role in defining property rights in the United States and in adding value to the land. Although technically trespassers on the public domain, these squatters possessed, in the words of Donald Pisani, a 'law-mindedness rooted in the conviction that . . . "the people" have a greater right to define and interpret the rules than legal experts'.[109] To this end, the extralegal organizations performed a range of functions, from negotiating with the government to registering the properties and rights that squatters claimed.

Claim Associations

The claim associations of the American Midwest were originally formed by settlers to protect their rights against speculators or claim jumpers. Two claim associations in Iowa, for example, agreed in their constitutions to protect each member's claims for a period of two years after the land sales.[110] Allan Bogue, a historian of these Iowa 'claim clubs', notes that 'the squatter could expect that his comrades in the club would come to his assistance if claim jumpers threatened his holding and . . . his friends would intimidate speculators who might seek to outbid him at the land auction'.[111] One local Iowa historian noted that

> when an actual settler – one who wanted land for a home and immediate occupancy . . . settled on a portion of [an association's] domain, he was immediately set upon by the bloodhounds, and it was demanded of him that he either abandon the claim or pay them for [what] they maintained was their right . . .[If] the settler expressed doubt to their having previously claimed their site, the [claim association] always had one or more witnesses at hand to testify to the validity of the interest they asserted.[112]

These associations provided their own strict and primitive justice. A local minister once asked an association member what would happen if a claim jumper succeeded in buying his claims. The squatter replied: 'Why, I'll kill him; and, by agreement of the settlers, I am to be protected, and if tried, no settler dare, if on the jury find a verdict against me.'[113] More typically, however, claim associations provided at least the illusion of due process, by convening juries – of fellow-squatters – to sit in on cases of claim jumpers. In one Iowa county a claim jumper who attempted to occupy a vacant second tract owned by a member of a claim association was 'within an hour' brought by 'a score of earnest, angry men' before a settler jury.[114]

But the function of their claim associations also extended beyond protection against third parties all the way into the official law. For example, members of the associations, 'usually the squatters who first took up land in an area, agreed not to bid against each other at land auctions and to prevent others from bidding against [association] members'.[115] One claim association's constitutional preamble candidly describes its mission:

> Whereas, we have, by the sanction of the Government become settlers on its lands, and have expended out time and money in improving them, we feel justly entitled to buy them at the regular price. And whereas there may be persons disposed to interfere with our rights, and thus create distrust, excitement, and alarm; Therefore it is Resolved, that in our case there is safety, only in Union – and a determination to settle amicably any disputes amongst us, to reciprocate concessions, and avoid every thing, that may have a tendency to create distrust and excitement – to abide explicitly by the wards of the several committees, and defend them in the discharge of the duties assigned to them.[116]

This document is particularly striking in its resemblance to the 'settlement contracts' that groups of squatters make throughout much of the Third World today.

Each claim association drafted its own constitution and by-laws, elected operating officers, established rules for adjudicating disputes and established a procedure for the registration and protection of claims.[117] The constitution of the claim association of Johnson County, Iowa, for example, provided for a president, vice-president, clerk and recorder; for the election of seven judges, any five of whom could compose a court and settle disputes; for the election of two marshals charged with enforcing rules of the association; and for procedures that specified property rights in land.[118] According to Allan Bogue, most of 'the regulations covered the size of the

claims allowed; direction for marking, registering, and transferring claims; and the procedure to be followed when club
members contested each other's rights, when members were
threatened by claim jumpers, and when the date of the land
sale arrived'.[119]

The settlement contracts of the claim associations clearly
worked to increase the value of land that squatters claimed. In
the Iowa counties of Poweshiek, Johnson and Webster claim
associations drafted specific 'regulations prescribing the degree
to which the member must improve his claim'.[120] Associations
also set upper and lower limits upon the size of the claim to be
protected, and most allowed members to sell their claims in
order to capture their property's value. Many members, however, 'were not content with the amount of land the law
entitled them to, but made pretended claims to so large a
portion of the territory, that in some instances, it was difficult
for a buyer to find an unclaimed lot'.[121] This practice had the
tacit support of most association members. Although members
of claim associations denounced large speculators, they themselves were, as White points out, 'small-scale speculators'.[122]
The claim associations of American history were more than
just a scheme to protect the homestead; they were used to protect the *trade* in claims.[123]

And thus claim associations helped create 'a kind of
common-law . . . established by common consent, and common necessity'.[124] As Tatter further pointed out, 'although
claim-law is no law derived from the United States, or from the
statute book of the territory yet it nevertheless is the law, made
by and derived from the sovereigns themselves, and its
mandates are imperative'.[125] The settlers, however, did not
displace official law completely. Their extralegal arrangements
served as temporary rest stops on the road to legal
respectability.

Miners' Organizations

On 24 January 1848 James Marshall and a group of Indians and Mormons discovered gold along California's American River. Although the miners swore an oath of secrecy, within four months word of their discovery had reached the San Francisco newspapers. This discovery 'sparked probably the greatest voluntary human migration in world history to that time in a rush to California for gold'.[126] The immediate effect was profound: 'Farmers left their plows in the fields. Soldiers and sailors deserted. Shopkeepers abandoned their business. San Francisco became a ghost town over night.'[127] Within one year there were 100,000 miners in California; two years later almost 300,000.

When these hopeful prospectors rushed into California to strike it rich they 'found no fences, no surveyor's corners'.[128] Nevertheless, legally, they were trespassers since most of the land they were prospecting had hundreds of competing interests.[129] At the time of the gold rush, most of the land was owned by the federal government, up to 9 per cent of the total area of California was covered by Mexican land grants, while much of the rest was desert, mountainous or otherwise inaccessible.[130] And in spite of the fact that the federal government was, as we have seen, churning out hundreds of statutes regulating land use, the United States had no law regulating the sale or lease of federal lands containing precious minerals.[131] Moreover, Congress explicitly excluded 'mineral lands' from the general pre-emption act of 1841.

The combustible nexus of Mexican land grants, absentee owners and land-hungry settlers and the absence of a federal law that could be enforced created the immediate need for extralegal arrangements. Historians such as Pisani felt the settlers did not have much choice: if 'they settled on a Mexican claim in the hope it would be disallowed, they faced the prospect of losing their improvements. But if they purchased land from a claimant whose boundaries were subsequently adjusted, or whose application was subsequently rejected, they might lose the cost of the land as well as the value of their improvements.'[132] While the settlers made their own arrangements, the government tried to find a solution based on existing official law. The problem was that the government was far too slow. In 1851 Congress established a commission to pass judgement on the validity of the Mexican and Spanish land grants. Although the commission's official tenure lasted until 1856, the courts and the General Land Office put off final action until years later. The result was that the settlers had to rely increasingly on their extralegal law to maintain some sense of order. They were forced to, because, in the words of Pisani: 'The longer the confirmation process took, the greater chance of litigation and violence.'[133]

Like the claim club squatters in the Midwest, miners had two precedents on their side: the right of pre-emption and the right of occupants to their improvements.[134] So they formed organizations to regulate their extralegal rights and stipulate the obligations that individual miners had to the invaded lands. These settlement contracts were known as 'mining district regulations'. The miners knew that if they drafted their regulations carefully, with as much regard as possible for existing law, sooner or later the government would have to come to terms with them.

The miners left little to chance. Most mining district regulations generally involved nine distinct stages. First, the miners posted notices or got the word out announcing a mass meeting at a well-known location to form a new district. Second, as the meeting's first order of business, the miners established the boundaries and jurisdiction of the district and named it (typically for some geographic feature of the area, for the first claim staked, or in honour of the man organizing the district). Third, the miners placed restrictions on ownership to the number of claims held by location and purchase. In most mining districts the discoverer of a new lode was normally allowed a double claim while others were allowed one per person. There was usually no limit on claims that were purchased, provided the purchase had been made 'upon good faith for valuable consideration with recorded deeds and certificates of ownership issued by the recorder'.

Fourth, the mining districts limited membership and rights to US citizens or those entitled under law to become citizens. Mexicans and Asians were thus generally excluded by the racial prejudices of the day. Mexican or Asian miners were even accused of having contributed 'nothing to the prosperity of the people whose hard-earned wealth they have appropriated to themselves' and of endangering the morals of 'young [American] men . . . without home influences'. Fifth, the regulations fixed the dimensions of the mining claim itself from 150 to 300 feet in length for large claims to the size of the miner's shovel for smaller diggings. A right-of-way was usually given on each side of the claim to run tunnels and drifts at any distance so long as they did not interfere with the rights of a neighbour's claim. Sixth, the regulations set guidelines for how miners would identify the boundaries of their claims. Usually, the claim was initiated by posting a dated notice of the claim with the names of the locator, the district and the county.

Seventh, the regulations established the office of the recorder, where the official records of the district would be kept, and specified how claims would be recorded. Often recorders were elected for a year. Even more importantly, the regulations required miners 'to file their notices of action with the recorder within five to thirty days from the date of posting on the claim, and the recorder was required to keep a book of such filing and also record transfers of titles within the district'. Eighth, the regulations established the requirements for development of claims by providing for the 'time, extent, and character' of work to be done in order to hold a claim. The 'penalty for noncompliance was always the possibility of forfeiture'. Finally, the regulations established a system for resolving disputes.[135]

Faced with a legal vacuum in federal mining law, the miners, with some legal acumen, created a kind of acting mining law. Negotiating among themselves, they worked to protect their rights and increase the value of their property until the government could step in to validate their claims. Creating property rights through extralegal means was hardly a rarity. Extralegality was – as it is today in the Third World – rife. In the immediate years after gold was discovered California had some eight hundred separate jurisdictions, each with its individual regulations.[136] Every jurisdiction obtained its initial legitimacy and strength from the consensus of its members. Charles Howard Shinn notes that 'no *alcalde* [mayor], no council, no justice of the peace was ever forced upon a district by an outside power. The district was the unit of political organization, in many regions, long after the creation of the state; and delegates from adjoining districts often met in consultation regarding boundaries, or matters of local government, and reported to their respective constituencies in open-air-meeting, on hillside or river-bank.'[137]

Eventually most politicians supported the miners' claims, and the courts proceeded to sanction their extralegal arrangements. In 1861 a justice of the California Supreme Court commented on the legitimacy of the miners' extralegal arrangements in *Gore v. McBreyer*: 'it is enough that the miners agree – whether in public meeting or after due notice – upon their local laws, and that these are recognized as the rules of the vicinage, unless some fraud be shown, or some other like cause for rejecting the laws'.[138]

One reason for the easy acceptance of miners' district regulations was that these were often drafted on the basis of principles, ideas and procedures not much different from those of existing official law. Lacy points out that the district regulations 'reflected the accumulated wisdom and customs . . . of the Stannary Convocations of the tin miners of Cornwall; the High Peak District practices and the Barmote Court of Derbyshire; the organization and practices of the Burger-meisters of Saxony; the Spanish Colonial ordinances of the vice royalties of New Spain and Peru; and some practices of the mining districts of the Missouri lead belt'.[139] For instance, 'where a miner took up his claim pursuant to mining rules and customs, actual possession of part of a claim with definite boundaries gave him a possessory right to the entire claim. This would seem to be little more than an application of . . . [an aspect] of the law of adverse possession.'[140] One lawyer for the miners discussed how their law paralleled and simplified the formal property rights system:

> Under the miners' law, the locator is his own executive officer to take the land, grant himself a possessory title, fix the boundaries, and announce himself the proprietor . . . The notice is the substitute for the written application; the marking of the boundaries answers the purpose of a survey; the mining law is the concession, and the record with the local officer the registration. The only official in charge is the great public, whom the miners represent, and whose law is inexorable.[141]

This fusion of informal and existing legal models filled the vacuum of formal law on America's vast mineral lands – just as squatting organizations do today in the Third World. During the 1850s Congress made no effort to take over the Western mineral resources. Historians speculate that perhaps the miners' success at self-government appealed to the political philosophy of the day, or maybe the nation was too preoccupied with the slavery issue and the threat of secession by the Southern states.[142] Perhaps the lawyers among the US legislators simply recognized good lawmaking when they saw it. One thing, however, is clear: the lack of congressional action only added credibility to the social contract that the miners themselves had not only devised but made work.[143]

By the 1860s, however, the Civil War, the need for funds with which to conduct it and investor concerns in California, Nevada and Colorado forced Congress to consider consolidating the thousands of mining laws into an integrated system.

The concerns of investors about land title played a prominent role in this debate. One contemporary noted that because of the lack of a standard system of titles 'capitalists were not willing to expend their money in sinking costly shafts, and erecting machinery and buildings, to prove a vein which by miners' law might be indefinitely subdivided according to its richness'.[144] The federal government seriously began to consider ways that it could regulate mining on federal land.[145] According to Lacy, one of the main concerns of members of Congress from the West was the 'clamor for security of title and the ability to purchase mineral lands at a reasonable price'.[146]

In 1866 Congress for the first time declared the nation's mineral lands officially open for exploration to US citizens – eighteen years after hundreds of thousands of miners had first begun to prospect for gold in federal lands in California. The 1866 statute explicitly noted that all explorations for minerals would be subject to those 'local customs or rules of miners in the several mining districts' that were not in conflict with the laws of the United States.[147] The purpose of the law was not to destroy rights borne extralegally but to strengthen them 'with some wholesome regulations as to the manner of holding and working them, which are not in conflict with existing mining laws, but simply give uniformity and consistency to the whole system'.[148] Another significant aspect of this premier mining law was that 'the substance of the bill came directly from the lode mining regulations of the Grass Valley Mining District of Nevada County, California ... and the Gold Mountain Mining District of Storey County, Nevada'.[149] In passing the law Congress went so far as to commend the American genius for creating extralegal arrangements:

> It is essential that this great system established by the people in their primary capacities, and evidencing by the highest possible testimony the peculiar genius of the American people for founding empire and order, shall be preserved and affirmed. Popular sovereignty is here displayed in one of its grandest

aspects, and simply invites us, not to destroy, but to put upon it the stamp of national power and unquestioned authority.[150]

And so the 1866 legislation not only acknowledged the legitimacy of social contracts born outside the official law, but incorporated principles and rights that had been won by settlers in pre-emption and settlement claims. The law also extended patent rights to any person or association that had expended $1,000 in labour and improvements on a claim, surveyed or unsurveyed. This was an explicit recognition that value added to assets was something the law needed to encourage and protect.

On 10 May 1872, Congress passed the general mining law, establishing a basic formal structure of American mining law that continues to this day. This law retained the two most important principles of the 1866 act: the recognition of miners' laws and the right of anyone who improved a mine to purchase the title from the government at a reasonable price.[151] In a span of twenty years the extralegally generated rights and arrangement of miners had been integrated into a new formal system. Even the Supreme Court, whose hostility to informal rights sparked a pro-squatter backlash, reaffirmed the validity of the 1866 and 1872 federal mining laws in *Jennison v. Kirk*. According to the Court, the two statutes 'gave the sanction of the government to possessory rights acquired under the local customs, laws, and decisions of the courts . . . [and] recognized the obligation of the government to respect private rights which had grown up under its tacit consent and approval. It proposed no new system, but sanctioned, regulated, and conferred a system already established, to which the people were attached.'[152] By the 1880s extralegal mining district rules and customs had been integrated into one coherent system of formal property law.[153]

At the end of the nineteenth century American politicians and judges had come a long way in the area of property law –

and it was the squatters who led them there. This was also true for housing: in 1862, when Congress passed the celebrated 'Homestead Act' that gave 160 free acres to any settler willing to live on the land for five years and develop it, it was only sanctioning what settlers had already done themselves.[154] In spite of the legendary fame of the Homestead Act, most settlement took place before it was enacted. 'Between 1862 and 1890, the population of the United States grew by 32 million people – but only about 2 million of them settled on the 372,649 farms claimed through the Homestead Act.'[155] By the time Congress finally approved it, the settlers already had many legal alternatives for gaining title to public lands.[156] Historically, however, the Homestead Act does have great symbolic value, signifying the end of a long, exhausting and bitter struggle between élitist law and a new order brought about by massive migration and the needs of an open and sustainable society. By ultimately embracing many of the extralegal arrangements of the settlers, formal law had legitimized itself, becoming the rule for most people in the United States rather than the exception.

The Significance for Third World and Former Communist Nations

For developing and ex-communist countries trying to make their own transition to capitalism, the American experience is extremely significant. The recognition and integration of extralegal property rights was a key element in the United States becoming the most important market economy and producer of capital in the world. As Gordon Wood emphasizes, during this time 'something momentous was happening in the society and culture that released the aspirations and energies of common people as never before in American history'.[157]

That 'momentous' something was a revolution in rights to property rights. The Americans, not always eagerly or consciously, gradually legitimized extralegal property norms and arrangements created by the poorest Americans and integrated them into the law of the land. At the beginning of the nineteenth century information about property and the rules that governed it were dispersed, atomized and unconnected. It was available in rudimentary ledgers, personal notes, informal constitutions and district regulations or oral testimony in every farm, mine or urban settlement. As in developing and former communist countries today, most of this information related only to the local community and was not available within any consistent network of systematized representations. Although American officials probably did not either intend or realize it, when they constructed national laws such as the pre-emption and mining acts they were creating the representational forms that integrated all this loose and isolated property data into a new formal property system.

It was not an easy task or a quick one; nor was it without violence. But the American experience is very much like what is going on today in Third World and former communist countries: the official law has not been able to keep up with popular initiative and government has lost control. As a result, people outside the West live today in a world of paradoxes similar to the one described by G. Edward White: 'When the miner left his shack and went to work, he employed the latest in industrial technology. When the farmer stepped outside his sod shanty, he often used the most modern farm machinery.'[158] Third Worlders also live and work in shacks and slums side by side with television sets and motor-powered tools. They, too, are organized in claim clubs. And their governments have also begun to give them pre-emption rights.

But what they still do not have is the efficiently crafted legal right to have their property integrated into a formal legal system that allows them to use it to create capital. Through occupancy, pre-emption, homesteading, miners' laws, and so on, Americans built a new concept of property, 'one that emphasized its dynamic aspects, associating it with economic growth', and which replaced a concept 'that emphasized its static character associating it with security from too rapid change'.[159] American property changed from being a means of preserving an old economic order to become, instead, a powerful tool for creating a new one. The result was the expanded markets and capital needed to fuel explosive economic growth. This was the 'momentous' change that still drives US economic growth.

Ultimately, the lessons of the United States' transition to formality will not be found in the technical details, but in changes in political attitudes and in broad legal trends. In passing laws to integrate the extralegal population, American politicians expressed the revolutionary idea that legal institutions can survive only if they respond to social needs.[160] The American legal system obtained its energy because it built on the experience of grassroots Americans and the extralegal arrangements they created, while rejecting those English common law doctrines that had little relevance to problems unique to the United States. In the long and arduous process of integrating extralegal property rights American legislators and jurists created a new system much more conducive to a productive and dynamic market economy. This process constituted a revolution borne out of the normative expectations of ordinary people, which the government developed into a systematized and professional formal structure.

This is not to say that developing and former communist nations should slavishly imitate the US transition. There are plenty of negative consequences in the US experience that they should be careful to avoid. But, as we have already seen, there is much to learn. The primary lesson is that pretending extralegal arrangements do not exist or trying to stamp them out, without a strategy to channel them into the legal sector, is a fool's errand – especially in the developing world, where, as we saw in Chapter 2, the extralegal sector now comprises the majority of the populations of those countries and holds trillions of dollars in dead capital.

Efforts to create a property revolution elsewhere in the Third World and ex-communist countries will face their own unique requirements, obstacles and opportunities. We must contend with other ongoing revolutions in communications, information technology and rapid urbanization, but the basic situation is the same. Today, in many developing and former communist nations, property law is no longer relevant to how the majority of people live and work. How can a legal system aspire to legitimacy if it cuts out 80 per cent of its people? The challenge is to correct this legal failure. The American experience shows that this is a threefold task: we must find the real social contracts on property, integrate them into the official law and craft a political strategy that makes reform possible. How governments can meet these challenges is the subject of the next chapter.

6

THE MYSTERY OF LEGAL FAILURE

Why Property Law Does Not Work Outside the West

The life of the law has not been logic; it has been experience.

US SUPREME COURT JUSTICE OLIVER WENDELL HOLMES

Nearly every developing and ex-communist nation has a formal property system. The problem is that most of their citizens cannot gain access to it. They have run into Fernand Braudel's bell jar, that invisible structure in the past of the West that reserved capitalism for a very small sector of society. Their only alternative, as we saw in Chapter 2, is to retreat with their assets into the extralegal sector where they can live and do business – but without ever being able to convert their assets into capital.

Before we can lift the bell jar, it is important to know that we will not be the first to try. As we shall see in this chapter, governments in developing countries have tried for 180 years to open up their property systems to the poor.

Why have they failed? The reason is that they usually operate under five basic misconceptions:

Δ   all people who take cover in the extralegal or underground sectors do so to avoid paying taxes;

Δ   real estate assets are not held legally because they have not been properly surveyed, mapped and recorded;

Δ   enacting mandatory law on property is sufficient, and governments can ignore the costs of compliance with that law;

Δ   existing extralegal arrangements or 'social contracts' can be ignored;

Δ   you can change something as fundamental as people's conventions on how they can hold their assets, both legal and extralegal, without high-level political leadership.

To explain these countries' underground economies, in which 50 to 80 per cent of the people typically operate, in terms of tax evasion is partially incorrect at best. Most people do not resort to the extralegal sector because it is a tax haven but because existing law, however elegantly written, does not address their needs or aspirations. In Peru, where my team designed the program for bringing small extralegal entrepreneurs into the legal system, some 276,000 of those entrepreneurs recorded their businesses *voluntarily* in new registry offices we set up to accommodate them – with no promise of tax reductions. Their underground businesses had paid no taxes at all. Four years later tax revenues from formerly extralegal businesses totalled US$1.2 billion.

We were so successful because we modified company and property law to adapt to the needs of entrepreneurs accustomed to extralegal rules. We also cut dramatically the costs of the red tape to enrol businesses. This is not to say that people do not care about their tax bill. But extralegal manufacturers and shopkeepers – who operate on razor-thin profit margins, in cents rather than dollars – know basic arithmetic. All we had to do was make sure the costs of operating legally were below those of surviving in the extralegal sector, facilitate the paperwork for legalization, make a strong effort to communicate the advantages of the programme, and then watch hundreds of thousands of entrepreneurs happily quit the underground.

Contrary to popular wisdom, operating in the underground is hardly cost-free. Extralegal businesses are taxed by the lack of good property law and continually having to hide their operations from the authorities. Because they are not incorporated, extralegal entrepreneurs cannot lure investors by selling shares; they cannot secure low-interest formal credit because they do not even have legal addresses; they cannot reduce risks by declaring limited liability or obtaining insurance coverage. The only 'insurance' available to them is that provided by their neighbours and the protection that local bullies or mafias are willing to sell them. Moreover, because extralegal entrepreneurs live in constant fear of government detection and extortion from corrupt officials, they are forced to split and compartmentalize their production facilities between many locations, thereby rarely achieving important economies of scale. In Peru 15 per cent of gross income from manufacturing in the extralegal sector is paid out in bribes, ranging from 'free samples' and special 'gifts' of merchandise to outright cash. With one eye always on the lookout for the police, underground entrepreneurs cannot openly advertise to build up their clientele or make less costly bulk deliveries to customers.

Our research has confirmed that in most countries being free from the costs and nuisance of the extralegal sector generally compensates for paying taxes. Whether you are inside the bell jar or outside, you will be taxed. What determines whether you remain outside is the relative cost of being legal.

Another prime misconception is that real estate assets cannot be legally registered unless they have been surveyed, mapped and recorded with state-of-the-art geomatic information technology. This, too, is at best partially true. Europeans and Americans managed to record all their real estate assets

decades before computers and geographical information systems were invented. As we saw in the last chapter, throughout
the nineteenth century the surveying of newly settled land in
the United States lagged many years behind the conveyance of
property rights. In Japan I examined the documentation available in registry offices and saw how some land assets had been
recorded after the Second World War using maps from the Edo
period – three to four centuries before the invention of aerial
photography and global positioning systems.

This does not mean that state-of-the-art computing and geographical information systems are not extremely important to
any government's efforts to open up its property system to the
poor. What it does mean is that the widespread under-
capitalization, informal squatting and illegal housing
throughout the non-Western world are hardly caused by a lack
of advanced information and mapping technology.

Braudel's bell jar is made not of taxes, maps and computers
but laws. What keeps most people in developing and former
communist nations from using modern formal property to
create capital is a bad legal and administrative system. Inside
the bell jar are élites who hold property using codified law
borrowed from the West. Outside the bell jar, where most
people live, property is used and protected by all sorts of
extralegal arrangements firmly rooted in informal consensus
dispersed through large areas. These local social contracts
represent collective understandings of how things are owned
and how owners relate to each other. Creating one national
social contract on property involves understanding the psy-
chological and social processes – the beliefs, desires, intentions,
customs and rules – that are contained in these local social
contracts and then using the tools that professional law provides to weave them into one formal national social contract.
This is what Western nations achieved not so long ago.

The crucial point to understand is that property is not a
physical thing that can be photographed or mapped. Property
is not a primary quality *of* assets, but the legal expression of

an economically meaningful consensus *about* assets. Law is the instrument that fixes and realizes capital. In the West the law is less concerned with representing the physical reality of buildings or real estate than with providing a process or rules that will allow society to extract potential surplus value from those assets. Property is not the assets themselves but a consensus between people as to how those assets should be held, used and exchanged. The challenge today in most non-Western countries is not to put all the nation's land and buildings into the same map (which has probably already been done) but to integrate the formal legal conventions inside the bell jar with the extralegal ones outside it.

No amount of surveying and mapping will accomplish this. No amount of computerizing will convert assets into a form that allows them to enter expanded markets and become capital. As we saw in Chapter 3, assets themselves have no effect on social behaviour: they do not produce incentives, they make no person accountable, no contract enforceable. Assets are not intrinsically 'fungible' – capable of being divided, combined or mobilized to suit any transaction. All of these qualities grow out of modern property law. It is law that detaches and fixes the economic potential of assets as a value separate from the material assets themselves and allows humans to discover and realize that potential. It is law that connects assets into financial and investment circuits. And it is the representation of assets fixed in legal property documents that gives them the powers to create surplus value.

More than sixty years ago, the eminent legal historian C. Reinold Noyes wrote:

> The chips in the economic game today are not so much the physical goods and actual services that are almost exclusively considered in economic text books, as they are that elaboration of legal relations which we call property . . . One is led, by studying its development, to conceive the social reality as a web of intangible bonds – a cobweb of invisible filaments – which

> surround and engage the individual and which thereby
> *organize* society . . . And the process of coming to grips with
> the actual world we live in is the process of objectivizing these
> relations.[1]

Lifting the bell jar, then, is principally a legal challenge. The official legal order must interact with extralegal arrangements outside the bell jar to create a social contract on property and capital. To achieve this integration, many other disciplines are, of course, necessary: economists have to get the costs and numbers right; urban planners and agronomists must assign priorities; mappers, surveyors and computer experts are indispensable to make the information systems work. But, ultimately, an integrated, national social contract will be concretized only in laws. All other disciplines play only a supporting role.

Does that mean that lawyers should lead the integration process? No. Implementing major legal change is a political responsibility. There are various reasons for this. First, law is generally concerned with protecting property rights, but the real task in developing and ex-communist countries is not so much to perfect existing rights as to give everyone a right to property rights – 'meta-rights', if you will. Bestowing such meta-rights, emancipating people from bad law, is a political job. Second, very small, but powerful, vested interests – mostly represented by the countries' best commercial lawyers – are likely to oppose change unless they are convinced otherwise. Bringing well-connected and moneyed people on to the bandwagon requires not consultants committed to serving their clients but talented politicians committed to serving their people. Third, creating an integrated system is not about drafting laws and regulations that look good on paper, but rather about designing norms that are rooted in people's beliefs and are thus more likely to be obeyed and enforced. Being in touch with real people is a politician's task. Fourth, prodding underground economies to become legal is a major political sales job. Governments must convince poorer citizens – who mistrust government and survive on tight parochial arrangements – and some of the mafias who protect them to buy an entry ticket into a much bigger and looser game. Governments must also convince influential leftists, who in many countries are close to the grassroots, that enabling their constituencies to produce capital is the best way to help them. Citizens inside and outside the bell jar need government to make a strong case that a redesigned, integrated property system is less costly, more efficient and better for the nation than the existing anarchical arrangements.

Without succeeding on these legal and political fronts, no nation can overcome the legal apartheid between those who can create capital and those who cannot. Without formal property, no matter how many assets they accumulate or how hard they work, most people will not be able to prosper in a capitalist society. They will continue to remain beyond the radar of policy-makers, out of the reach of official records, and thus economically invisible.

Western governments succeeded in lifting the bell jar, but it was an erratic, unconscious process that took hundreds of years. My colleagues and I have synthesized what we think they did right into a formula we call the 'capitalization process', with which we are assisting various governments throughout the world (see Figure 6.1). Explaining the details is not part of this book, but readers who would like a technical description of the entire plan are invited to consult unpublished documentation in Institue for Liberation and Democracy archives. In the rest of this chapter I will focus on the two indispensable components of the formula: the legal challenge (A.4 in Figure 6.1) and the political challenge (B.1 in Figure 6.1).

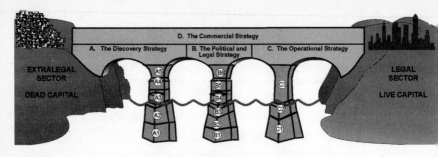

Figure 6.1
CAPITALIZATION PROCESS
MOVEMENT FROM DEAD CAPITAL TO LIVE CAPITAL

A. THE DISCOVERY STRATEGY

    A.1   Identify, locate and classify extralegal assets (dead capital)

    A.1.1   Develop local recruitment specifications to penetrate extralegal sector.

    A.1.2   Determine causes for the accumulation of extralegal assets so as to develop workable typologies.

    A.1.3   Locate economic sectors and geographic areas where extralegal activities are most prevalent.

    A.2   Quantify the actual and potential value of extralegal assets (dead capital)

    A.2.1   Develop appropriate methodologies to estimate the value of extralegal assets using existing information and data gathered in the field.

    A.2.2   Customize criteria to gather and process information and to confirm results.

    A.2.3   Establish the importance of the value of extralegal assets.

    A.3   Analyze the interaction of the extralegal sector with the rest of society

    A.3.1   Research the relevant links between government and extralegal assets.

    A.3.2   Research the relevant links between legal businesses and extralegal assets.

    A.3.3   Identify processes where government has already successfully dealt with extralegal assets.

    A.4   Identify the extralegal norms that govern extralegal property

    A.4.1   Detect and decode the extralegal norms that define the manner in which property rights are held and exercised by the different extralegal communities in the country.

    A.5   Determine the costs of extralegality to the country

    A.5.1   The costs to the extralegal sector

    A.5.2   The costs to the legal business sector

    A.5.3   The costs to government

B. THE POLITICAL AND LEGAL STRATEGY

    B.1   Ensure that the highest political level assumes responsibility for capitalization of the poor

    B.2   Put into operation agencies that will permit rapid change

    B.2.1   Identify and connect with the capitalization process the different institutions that presently govern property rights or impinge upon their ability to generate surplus value.

    B.2.2   Design, obtain approval for, and put into operation agencies that will permit the rapid introduction of changes in the diverse processes required for capitalization. If possible, create a single organization having the sole mandate of capitalizing assets and decentralize offices to provide services throughout the country.

    B.2.3   Ensure that the capitalization process both incorporates the political priorities of the government and reflects a consensus within society that makes the process easily enforceable.

    B.3   Remove administrative and legal bottlenecks

    B.3.1   Calculate the costs of capitalizing extralegal assets, including:

    B.3.1.1 Requirements for permits at all levels of government.

    B.3.1.2 Requirements for and the amount of payments for these permits.

    B.3.1.3 The number of forms and other documents required.

    B.3.1.4 Requirements that cannot be met in practice.

    B.3.1.5 All other transaction costs, including time delays.

    B.3.2   Remove administrative and legal bottlenecks by identifying and modifying the institutions, statutes and practices that create unnecessary red tape.

    B.4   Build consensus between legal and extralegal sectors

    B.4.1   Determine the points where extralegal norms coincide with the law so as to be able to draft statutes that recognize acceptable extralegal proofs of ownership with the support of extralegal communities.

    B.4.2   Ensure that the draft legal norms that incorporate extralegal property do so without compromising the level of security that the existing legal order now provides property that is duly recorded and effectively controlled so as to obtain acquiescence of the legal sector.

    B.5   Draft statutes and procedures that lower the costs of holding assets legally below those of holding them extralegally

    B.5.1   Enact the statutes required for all property in a country to be governed by one consistent body of law and set of procedures.

    B.5.2   Broaden the definition of proofs of ownership to suit the new process, and consolidate into administratively manageable packages the statutes and procedures that will govern the capitalization process.

    B.5.3   Consolidate dispersed legislation into a single law.

    B.5.4   Develop institutions and procedures that permit economies of scale for all the activities which constitute the process of capitalization.

B.5.5 Create an expedient and low-cost alternative to squatting and other forms of extralegal appropriation. Consolidate process and respect for the law by establishing incentives and disincentives aimed at encouraging legal and discouraging illegal [extralegal] conveyance.

B.5.6 Design and implement administrative or private processes, to substitute judicial processes, where suitable, so as to encourage settlement of disputes within the law.

B.6 Create mechanisms that will reduce risks associated with private investment, including credibility of titles and non-payment for public

C. THE OPERATIONAL STRATEGY

C.1 Design and implement field operation strategy, procedures, personnel, equipment, offices, training and manuals that enable government to recognize and process individual property rights in the extralegal sector

C.1.1 Design mechanisms to obtain the massive participation of the members of extralegal settlements for the purpose of reducing the costs of capitalization.

C.1.2 Carry out training courses for the organization of capitalization brigades that reflect the types of extralegality they will encounter.

C.1.3 Develop manuals that explain to the leaders and the people of extralegal settlements the ways in which they can participate in the selection and collection of proofs of ownership.

C.1.4 Prepare for capitalizing extralegal communities

C.1.4.1 Identify and train local promoters within each community

C.1.4.2 Implement a local promotional campaign within each community

C.1.4.3 Educate each community about the proofs of ownership required

C.1.4.4 Train local leaders to record ownership information on registration forms

C.1.4.5 Identify and train private verifiers to certify information collected by the community.

C.1.5 Gather and process information on physical assets.

C.1.5.1 Obtain or prepare maps showing the boundaries of individual parcels (where necessary prepare digital base maps to record boundary information)

C.1.5.2 Verify that maps showing individual parcels correspond with what is on the ground

C.1.5.3 Enter the maps into the computer system.

C.1.6 Gather and process ownership information.

C.1.6.1 Gather ownership information and record on registration forms

C.1.6.2 Verify that ownership rights are valid under the new law

C.1.6.3 Enter the ownership information into the computer system

C.1.6.4 Officially register the ownership rights

C.1.6.5 Hand out certificates to the beneficiaries at a public ceremony.

C.2 Implement communications strategies using appropriate media to encourage participation of the extralegal sector, support in the business community and the government sector, and acquiescence among those with vested interests in the status quo

C.2.1 Conduct a campaign for each particular type of community in the extralegal sector to encourage their participation in the process.

C.2.2 Devise mechanisms that show beneficiaries of capitalization process that their assets are protected by the same institutional framework that protects the rights of private investors, both domestic and foreign. This will give these owners a reason to respect contracts governed by the formal legal order.

C.2.3 Conduct a campaign for each legal community that may feel vulnerable.

C.2.4 Design the means of communicating to legal sector the benefits of capitalization, emphasizing the reduction in risks and making it clear that capitalization will neither affect existing property rights nor compromise the rights of third parties.

C.2.5 Conduct a campaign for professionals with vested interests in property definition, explaining their future role and increased involvement within an expanded legal sector after capitalization.

C.3 Re-engineer the record keeping organizations and registration processes so that they can pull together all the economically useful descriptions about a country's extralegal assets and integrate them into one data/knowledge based computer system

C.3.1 Structure the organization of the registry and its internal work flows, simplify the registration processes, establish specifications for automating information, design and implement a quality control system, select and train personnel, and establish procedures to ensure that the registry can handle a massive national program of capitalization.

C.3.2 Construct GIS based systems to provide spatial analytical capabilities.

C.3.3 Establish control mechanisms to guarantee that the cost of enrollment and registration services are sufficiently efficient and cost effective that its users will not be motivated to slip back into extralegality.

C.3.4 Insert descriptions of features of extralegal property holdings into customized, computer-friendly registration forms where they can be differentiated, recorded and managed in one computer environment.

C.3.5 Break down the information that is traditionally contained in deeds into simple categories that can be entered into computer software and be systematized for easy access, after having effected a legally approved stream-lining of existing information gathering procedures.

C.3.6 Facilitate the update of computerized property information by placing data input centers close to the beneficiaries. The purpose is to cut down on the transportation and transaction costs of legally registering property and property-related business and keeping their status legal.

D. THE COMMERCIAL STRATEGY

D.1 Implement the information and enforcement mechanisms that will enable the provision of:

D.1.1 **Banking/Mortgages/Credit**

D.1.2 **Public Utilities**
(Energy, water, sewage, telecommunications)

D.1.3 **Collection Systems**
(Credit, rates, taxes)

D.1.4 **Databases/Information Services**

D.1.5 **Insurance products**
(Property damage, life insurance, credit insurance, liens, title insurance)

D.1.6 **National Identification Systems**

D.1.7 **Housing and Infrastructure**

D.1.8 **National Security**

PART I:
The Legal Challenge

As things stand, the creation of one integrated property system in non-Western nations is impossible. Extralegal property arrangements are dispersed among dozens, sometimes hundreds, of communities; rights and other information are known only to insiders or neighbours. All the separate, loose extralegal property arrangements characteristic of most Third World and former communist nations must be woven into a single system from which general principles of law can be drawn. In short, the many social contracts 'out there' must be integrated into one all-encompassing social contract.

How can this be accomplished? How can governments find out what the extralegal property arrangements are? That was precisely the question put to me by five members of the Indonesian cabinet. I was in Indonesia to launch the translation of my previous book into Bahasa Indonesian, and they took that opportunity to invite me to talk about how they could find out who owns what among the 90 per cent of Indonesians who live in the extralegal sector. Fearing that I would lose my audience if I went into a drawn-out technical explanation on how to structure a bridge between the extralegal and legal sectors, I came up with another way, an Indonesian way, to answer their question. During my book tour I had taken a few days off to visit Bali, one of the most beautiful places on earth. As I strolled through rice fields, I had no idea where the property boundaries were. But the dogs knew. Every time I crossed from one farm to another, a different dog barked. Those Indonesian dogs may have been ignorant of formal law, but they were positive about which assets their masters controlled.

I told the ministers that Indonesian dogs had the basic information they needed to set up a formal property system. By travelling their city streets and countryside and listening to the barking dogs, they could gradually work upwards, through the vine of extralegal representations dispersed throughout their country, until they made contact with the ruling social contract. 'Ah,' responded one of the ministers, 'Jukum Adat [the people's law]!'

Discovering 'the people's law' is how Western nations built their formal property systems. Any government that is serious about re-engineering the ruling informal agreements into one national formal property social contract needs to listen to its barking dogs. To integrate all forms of property into a unified system, governments must find out how and why the local conventions work and how strong they are. The failure to do so explains why past attempts at legal change in developing and former communist countries have not worked. People tend to look upon the 'Social Contract' as an invisible, god-like abstraction that resides only in the minds of visionaries like Locke, Hume and Rousseau. But my colleagues and I have discovered that the social contracts of the extralegal sector are not merely implied social obligations that can be inferred from societal behaviour; they are also arrangements that are explicitly documented by real people. As a result, these extralegal social contracts can be touched, and they can also be assembled to build a property and capital formation system that will be recognized and enforced by society itself.

The Move from a Pre-capitalist to a Capitalist Property System

Without an integrated formal property system, a modern market economy is inconceivable. Had the advanced nations of the West not integrated all representations into one standardized property system and made it accessible to all, they could not have specialized and divided labour to create the expanded market network and capital that have produced their present wealth. The inefficiencies of non-Western markets have a lot to do with the fragmentation of their property arrangements and the unavailability of standard representations. This lack of integration restricts interaction not only between the legal and the extralegal sector but among the poor themselves. Extralegal communities do interchange with each other, but only with great difficulty. They are like flotillas of ships that remain in formation by navigating with reference to each other rather than to some common and objective standard, such as the stars or the magnetic compass.

Common standards in one body of law are necessary to create a modern market economy.[2] As C. Reinold Noyes has pointed out:

> Human nature demands regularity and certainty and this demand requires that these primitive judgements be consistent and thus be permitted to crystallize into certain rules – into 'this body of dogma or systematized prediction which we call law' ... The practical convenience of the public ... leads to the recurrent efforts to systematize the body of laws. The demand for codification is a demand of the people to be released from the mystery and uncertainty of unwritten or even of case law.[3]

To make the transition from a condition where people already rely on a diversity of extralegal practices established by mutual consent to one codified legal system is a daunting challenge. As we have seen, this is what the nations of the West had to do to move from pre-capitalist 'primitive judgements' to a systematized body of laws. That is how they lifted their bell jars. However, as successful as those nations have been, they were not always conscious of what they were doing and left behind no clear blueprint. Even in Britain, eager to extend the benefits of the Industrial Revolution, reform efforts went on for almost a full century (from 1829 to 1925) before the government was in a position to make sure that real estate assets could be centrally recorded and easily transferred. John C. Payne sums up how difficult and erratic property reform was for England:

A great many statutes were passed, and English property law was made over from top to bottom. Much of this reform was *ad hoc* improvisation, and one gets the impression that the leaders of the movement did not always have a clear idea of what they were doing or why they were doing it. English land law had become so technical and had gained so many accretions through the centuries that the task must initially have seemed almost overwhelming. The difficulty was that there was so much detail to be attended to that it was hard to get to the heart of the matter. So the English reformers began to strike about them with all good will but with more energy than clarity of concept. In the long run they did their work well, but it took them a century to do it, and in the interim they attempted many unsuccessful experiments and were ultimately forced into a number of compromises.[4]

The Failure of Mandatory Law

One might assume that today it would be relatively easy for developing and former communist nations to lift their bell jars. After all, the right of universal access to property is now recognized by nearly every national constitution in the world and by many international conventions. Programs to endow the poor with property exist in almost all developing and former communist countries. Whereas the reforms of the West during the eighteenth and nineteenth centuries encountered widespread intellectual and moral resistance against sharing formal property rights, access to property is today considered part and parcel of the fundamental rights of humankind. A wide array of contemporary international treaties, ranging from the Universal Declaration of Human Rights of 1948 and the catechism of the Catholic Church to the 169th Covenant of the International Labour Office on Indigenous and Tribal People in Independent Countries of 1989, insist on property as a basic and stable human right. In different degrees courts and laws all over the world see this right as an important legal principle. The invading army's age-old custom of plundering property has been explicitly forbidden by international law since the International Convention of The Hague of 1899. International law thus treats the property rights of individuals as more sacred than the sovereign rights of states, providing that even if governments lose lands, property owners in those same territories shall not lose theirs.

The United States, Canada, Japan and Europe – the twenty-five developed nations of the world – have prospered so much more than those without their kind of accessible, integrated formal property systems that today no one would seriously propose economic solutions that disregarded the need for formal property. That is why most developing and former communist nations today recognize the principle of universal access to property rights as a political necessity as well as an implicit ingredient of their macroeconomic and market reform programs.

The political intention to legalize the assets of the poor has been consecrated in Latin American law for nearly two centuries. The first Peruvian Constitution, written in 1824, just two years after independence from Spain, clearly stated that the poor, then mostly Peruvians of native origin, were the legitimate owners of their land. When it nevertheless became obvious that Peru's élites were gradually dispossessing the indigenous poor, the government enacted over the years a series of laws reinforcing the intent of the Peruvian Constitution. None of them worked. The indigenous people got statutes that generally confirmed that their assets were legally theirs. What they did not get were the mechanisms that would have allowed them to fix the economic rights over their assets in representations protected by law.

The reason is now very clear: in Peru (and many other countries outside the West) most legal procedures to create formal property are not geared to process extralegal proofs of ownership that lack any visible chain of title – which, of course, is the only kind of proof the poor have. Nor can existing law follow and record subsequent changes in an asset's title as transactions continue to modify property relationships over time. As we saw in Chapter 2, today, in the best of circumstances, with modern maps, computers, human rights organizations standing by and all the best intentions in the world, legal procedures for recording titles and changes to them can take twenty years. From the evidence we have uncovered, it seems that Peruvian natives in the nineteenth century faced delays that were no better and probably worse. For people up against such obstacles, creating extralegal rules to protect their assets was the only rational thing to do.

When it became clear that the mandatory laws were not helping the indigenous people of Peru concretize their rights, the economic élites swung back into action, dreaming up new tricks to circumvent the laws' intent. Where official titles did not exist, the well connected and their lawyers began inventing them, reconstituting the documentary evidence and getting local authorities and notaries to issue legal titles in their favour (*títulos supletorios*, as they were called). Once again the élite dispossessed indigenous Peruvians or forced them to sell on the cheap. The government, instead of investigating why the poor were not able to use the law for their benefit, assumed that the law was not the problem but that the poor were inherently inferior. So instead of improving the law, they extracted some of the poor from the mainstream law and its leveraging tools and built firewalls around their land. In 1924 Peru enacted a major law to protect natives from further legal ploys by packing thousands of them into rural farming communities where the transfer of rights to any land was expressly prohibited. In thus protecting the natives from the scheming and swindling élites, they also deprived them, albeit unintentionally, of the basic tools for creating capital.

These rural enclaves, however, could hold only a small percentage of the native population. By the late 1960s and early 1970s the remaining majority were still vulnerable and unhappy and, consequently, a potentially volatile class, especially with the sudden emergence of strong and well-organized leftist movements. To defuse this new threat, the Peruvian government, like those of many Third World countries, instituted agrarian reform programs that expropriated massive tracts of lands from large farms and ranches (*haciendas*) to create over six hundred government-run agrarian cooperatives for farmers. Again the aim was noble: to make sure that natives had access to real estate. What turned even these efforts into failures was that many of the indigenous people disliked working inside imposed bureaucracies. They broke up the cooperatives into private parcels of land and turned once again to more familiar and flexible extralegal arrangements to protect their newly established rights. What the government had not taken into account was that when people finally acquire property, they have their own ideas about how to use and exchange it. If the legal system does not facilitate the people's needs and ambitions, they will move out of the system in droves.

Peruvian history offers an important lesson for reformers of all political stripes. Government programs to give property to the poor have failed over the last 150 years whether they followed the bias of the right (private property rights through mandatory law) or of the left (protecting poor people's land in government-run collectives). The crippling political agendas of 'left *v.* right' are largely irrelevant to the needs of most people in developing countries. These people move out of the law not because the law has privatized or collectivized them but simply because it does not address what they want. Their wants may vary. Sometimes they need to combine their properties and sometimes they need to divide them. If the law does not help them, then they will help themselves outside the law. What characterizes the enemies of property and capital formation in developing and former communist countries is not whether they are leftists or rightists, but whether they are the friends of the status quo. Governments in developing countries need to stop living on the prejudices of Westerners hung up on the cruelty of enclosure and the creation of property in Britain centuries ago or on the bloody dispossession of Native Americans throughout the Americas. Those moral debts have to be paid in the West, not abroad. What governments elsewhere have to do is listen to the barking dogs in their own countries and find out what their law should say. Only then will people stop living outside it.

Formal law is increasingly losing its legitimacy as people continue to create property beyond its reach. Our data from abroad indicated that from the 1960s to the 1990s, the extralegal sector had grown larger not only in Peru but in other developing and ex-communist nations. Presuming that the failure of mandatory law was not only a Peruvian phenomenon, in 1994 I put together a special research team to find out if in the last thirty years international financial institutions had reported carrying out any successful and massive 'formalization' program in the Third World – one where all assets were properly represented and integrated into one system so as to produce capital. Despite months of methodically sifting through the records of the US Treasury and international organizations, we found nothing even remotely resembling the success of advanced nations.

What we did find was that over the past four decades various governments had started many such programs by earmarking billions of dollars to finance a huge array of property-related activities such as surveying, mapping and computerized recording systems. These projects had two main features in common: an extraordinary number of them had been prematurely aborted because of poor results ('Lots of new maps and computers, but few new formal owners,' reported one government project manager in Brazil); and, with the exception of some rural Thai property certification programmes, none of these efforts succeeded in turning extralegal assets into legal ones. We certainly found no evidence that assets were being transformed into capital.

Was it because governments did not really care? Certainly

not. In Peru, for instance, the government had tried to formalize property at least twenty-two times in the four hundred years since the Spanish conquest. Their success rate: zero. We called on titling authorities from other developing countries and obtained similar replies: major programs had failed or had only a marginal impact. Again, and significantly, nobody we talked to in those countries could claim that any consequential number of titles issued were fungible and fixed in such a way as to be part of an integrated network where capital formation could take place.

The evidence is overwhelming: no matter how hard developing and former communist nations have tried, no matter how good their intentions, there remains an enormous distance between what mandatory law commands and what has to be done for the law to work. Mandatory law is not enough. As Andrzej Rapaczynski has pointed out:

The notion that simply instituting an appropriate legal regime will establish a set of property rights that can undergird a modern economic system is deeply implausible, because most property rights can only be marginally enforced by the legal system. The core of the institution of ownership is a matter of unquestioned and largely unconscious social and economical practices that must be rooted in non-legal developments. This is the old Hobbesian problem: when most people obey the law, the government can enforce it effectively and [relatively] cheaply against the few individuals who break it. But when obedience breaks down on a large enough scale, no authority is strong enough to police everyone. In such a setting, with enforcement becoming less and less effective, individuals have an incentive to follow their own interests, regardless of any paper constraints.[5]

Throughout recent history, developing and former communist countries have not lacked political will, budgets, international manifestos or mandatory law drawn up with the explicit purpose of giving rights over assets to the majority of citizens. The problem is that when governments set out to ensure the property rights of poor people, they behave as if they were travelling to a place where there is a property vacuum, as if they were landing on the moon. They presume that all they have to do is fill this vacuum with mandatory law. In most cases, however, there is no vacuum. People already hold a huge amount of property through extralegal arrangements. While the assets of the poor may be outside the official law, their rights to those assets are nevertheless governed by social contracts of their own making. And when the mandatory law does not square with these extralegal conventions, the parties to those conventions will resent and reject the intrusion.

Rooting Law in the Social Contract

Extralegal social contracts on property underpin nearly all property systems and are part of the reality of every country, even in today's United States.[6] As Richard Posner has reminded us, property is socially constructed.[7] This means that property arrangements work best when people have formed a consensus about the ownership of assets and the rules that govern their use and exchange. Outside the West extralegal social contracts prevail for a good reason: they have managed much better than formal law to build on the consensus between people about how their assets ought to be governed. Any attempt to create a unified property system that does not take into account the collective contracts that underpin existing property arrangements will crash into the very roots of the rights most people rely on for holding on to their assets. Efforts to reform property rights fail because officials in charge of drafting new legal rules do not realize that most of their citizens have firmly established their own rules by social contract.

The notion that social contracts underlie successful laws goes all the way back to Plato, who thought that legitimacy had to be founded on some type of social contract. Even Immanuel Kant, in his statements against Locke, wrote that a social contract has to precede real ownership; all property rights spring from social recognition of a claim's legitimacy. To be legitimate, a right does not necessarily have to be defined by formal law; that a group of people strongly supports a particular convention is enough for it to be upheld as a right and defended against formal law.

That is why property law and titles imposed without reference to existing social contracts continually fail: they lack legitimacy. To obtain legitimacy, they have to connect with the extralegal social contracts that determine existing property rights. The problem, of course, is that these social contracts are dispersed throughout hundreds of extralegal jurisdictions in scattered villages and city neighbourhoods. The only organized way to integrate these social contracts into a formal property system is by building a legal and political structure, a bridge, if you will, so well anchored in people's own extralegal arrangements that they will gladly walk across it to enter this new, all-encompassing formal social contract. But this must be a bridge so solid that it does not crack and send everyone stampeding back into extralegal arrangements; a bridge so wide that no one falls from it. That is how, over hundreds of years, the West did it. Harold Berman reminds us:

> The systematization of law within various communities . . .
> was possible only because there had previously developed an
> informal structure of legal relations in those communities . . .
> The Western legal tradition grew – in the past – out of the
> structure of social and economic interrelationships within and
> among groups on the ground. Behavioral patterns of inter-
> relationship acquired normative dimensions: usages were
> transformed into custom . . . and custom into law.[8]

Building a legal and political bridge from social contracts scattered 'on the ground' into one national law is what Eugen Huber did in Switzerland at the turn of the twentieth century. Huber adjusted the Roman doctrines of Swiss statutory law to the customs, rules and behaviours dispersed throughout the cities, towns and farmland of his country. He pulled together all conventions on property into one codified law that secured the rights and obligations of people in line with the local norms to which they were accustomed. Huber liked to quote an old German saying, '*Das Gesetz muss aus dem Gedanken des Volkes gesprochensein*,' which, loosely translated, means, 'The law must come from the mouth of the people.' American law, as we saw in Chapter 5, showed the same respect for existing social contracts. Its strength was not its doctrinaire or professional coherence but its usefulness in the hands of authorities who wanted to transform undeveloped assets into productive ones.

The transitions from extralegal relations to unified formal property in advanced nations were not built on thin air. The systematization of the laws that underpin modern property rights structures was possible only because authorities allowed pre-existing extralegal relationships among groups on the ground sometimes to supersede official laws: 'Law both grows upward out of the structures and customs of the whole society,' wrote Berman, 'and moves downward from the policies and values of the rulers of society. Law helps to integrate the two.'[9]

By rooting formal property law in social contracts to which people were already committed, the governments of the West achieved the widespread popular acceptance required to overcome any resistance. The result was one legal system for property. With that in place, they were able to begin integrating dispersed conventions into one national social contract. And where once only the owner of a house and his neighbours could confirm whether the house belonged to him, with the advent of formal property the whole nation knew he was the owner. Formal property titles allowed people to move the fruits of their labour from a small range of validation into that of an expanded market. Western nations had thus laid out the energy plant to power a modern market and capitalist system.

Shifting the recognition of ownership from local arrangements into a larger order of economic and social relationships made life and business much easier. People no longer needed to rely on burdensome parochial politicking to protect their rights to assets. Formal property freed them from the time-consuming local arrangements inherent to closed societies. They could now control their assets. Even better, with adequate representations in hand, they could focus on their assets' economic potential. And because their real estate and businesses could now be located easily and identified nationally, owners lost their anonymity and became accountable. Gradually, these mechanisms of legal property set the stage for expanded markets and the creation of capital involving a huge number of players.

The Solidity of Pre-capitalist Social Contracts

Are the extralegal social contracts that prevail in developing countries today a solid enough foundation for creating official law? Without a doubt. There is a mountain of evidence that government officials implicitly and explicitly comply with the extralegal social contracts when they operate in the under-capitalized sector. Reports of international donor organizations refer continuously, albeit obliquely, to extralegal conventions. How could governments have developed agri-cultural and urban renewal projects in the poorest sections of their countries without coming to terms with extralegal beneficiary organizations? The fact that governments and international financial institutions help squatter settlements put in public services (roads, electricity, water and schools), in defiance of property law, is an implicit recognition of extralegal property arrangements. As Robert Cooter and Thomas Ulen have noted, 'the terms [of property rights] are often more efficient when people agree upon them than when a law-maker imposes them'.[10]

Extralegal social contracts rely on a combination of customs, *ad hoc* improvisations and rules selectively borrowed from the official legal system. In the absence of legal protection from the state in most developing nations it is extralegal law that regulates the assets of most citizens. This may sound oxymoronic or even subversive to Western readers who have come to believe there is only one law to obey. But my experience visiting and working in dozens of developing nations has made it clear to me that legal and extralegal laws coexist in all of them. As Margaret Gruter succinctly puts it:

> Law is ... not simply a set of spoken, written or formalized rules that people blindly follow. Rather, law represents the formalization of behavioral rules, about which a high percentage of people agree, that reflect behavioral propensities and that offer potential benefits to those who follow them. (When people do not recognize or believe in these potential benefits, laws are often disregarded or disobeyed ...)[11]

Another legal scholar has noted that the West's 'modern reliance on government to make law and establish order is not the historical norm'.[12] Diverse laws within one nation are nothing new. Legal pluralism ruled continental Europe until Roman law was rediscovered in the thirteenth and fourteenth centuries and all currents of law were gradually brought into one coordinated system.

We should not be surprised, then, to find that extralegal activity in developing and former communist countries is rarely haphazard. In the course of issuing formal title to hundreds of thousands of home and business owners in Peru my organization never found an extralegal group that did not comply with well-defined consensual rules. Whenever we visited an undercapitalized area, whether in Asia, America or the Middle East, we never stepped into a wilderness. By observing carefully, we were always able to distinguish patterns of rules. In the worst cases we found a neglected garden – never a jungle.

Like their Western predecessors, the undercapitalized sectors in the Third World and ex-communist countries have spontaneously generated their own varieties of property rules. To defend their incipient property rights from others, they have been forced to work out among themselves their own extralegal institutions. Remember, it is not your own mind that gives you certain exclusive rights over a specific asset, but other minds thinking about your rights in the same way you do. These minds vitally need each other to protect and control their assets. Moreover, people need to make their social contracts even stronger than formal law to fend off intruders, especially the government. Anyone doubting the strength of social contracts has only to challenge some of these extralegal rights. The resistance will be most impressive.

Extralegal arrangements have become astonishingly widespread over the past forty years. Reports about 'the mushrooming extralegal sector' seem as common as football scores in the newspapers of practically every Third World city. The reason is that formal law has not been able to accommodate rapidly evolving extralegal agreements. In real estate, for example, extralegal social contracts originate not only from outright squatting by migrants, but from deficient housing and urban or agrarian reform programs, the gradual deterioration of rent control programs, and the illegal purchase or lease of land for dwelling and industrial purposes. Most social contracts are facilitated by active agents: commercially, politically or religiously motivated 'real estate brokers' who have either something to gain from these transactions or a constituency to protect. The common denominator among their clients is that they cannot pay the costs of legally obtaining property. In some countries I have visited, branches of the armed forces appoint military officers to obtain real estate extralegally as living quarters for non-commissioned officers. More surprising still, I have seen municipal authorities in charge of real estate titling and registry operations organize informal squatting in order to provide their union members with decent land for their homes. One large squatter settlement I visited recently was initiated by the city council itself, to provide homes for some seven thousand families of government employees. In another country a local newspaper, intrigued by our evidence of extensive extralegal real estate holdings, checked to see if the head of state's official residence had a recorded title. It did not. The newspaper joked that the nation's laws were being enacted from an extralegal location.

Once rights to land have been created extralegally, those involved create institutions to administer the social contract they have built: informal business and residential organizations meet regularly, make decisions, obtain and supervise infrastructure investment, follow administrative procedure and issue credentials. They typically have a headquarters where maps and manual ledgers with ownership records may be found. The most striking feature of these institutions, throughout the world, is their desire to be integrated into the formal sector. In urban areas extralegal buildings and businesses evolve over time until they are barely distinguishable from property that is perfectly legal. In all developing and former communist nations I have visited a long frontier separates the legal from the extralegal. All along it there are checkpoints where extralegal organizations connect with government officials; where the former struggle to gain official acceptance and the latter try to achieve a semblance of order.[13] Usually, extralegal organizations will have worked out a way to coexist with some stratum of the government, probably at the municipal or local level. Most groups are trying to negotiate a legal niche to protect their rights, while others have already reached some sort of agreement that stabilizes their situation outside mainstream law. There is one other clue pointing to the fact that the extralegals want to come in from the cold: the engaging and diplomatic leaders they select to negotiate on their behalf hardly fit the stereotype of the street boss.

Listening to the Barking Dogs

Most governments of developing and former communist nations are probably ready to recognize that the reason why their extralegal sectors are growing exponentially is not because people have suddenly abandoned their respect for the law but because they have no alternative for protecting their property and earning a living. Once governments come to terms with this fact of modern life, they will have to strike a deal. Although the extralegals are already primed to cross the bridge into legal recognition, they will do so only if their governments make the trip easy, safe and cheap. Asset owners in the extralegal sector are already relatively well organized; they are also 'law-abiding', although the laws they abide by are not the government's. It is up to the government to find out what these extralegal arrangements are and then find ways to integrate them into the formal property system. But they will not be able to do that by hiring lawyers in high-rise offices in Delhi, Jakarta or Moscow to draft new laws. They will have to go out into the streets and roads, and listen to the barking dogs.

The law that prevails today in the West did not come from dusty tomes or official government statute books. It is a living entity, born in the real world and bred by ordinary people long before it got into the hands of professional lawyers. The law had to be discovered before it could be systematized. As the legal scholar Bruno Leoni reminds us:

> The Romans and the English shared the idea that the law is something to be *discovered* more than to be *enacted* and that

nobody is so powerful in his society as to be in a position to identify his own will with the law of the land. The task of 'discovering' the law was entrusted in their two countries to the jurist consult and to the judges, respectively – two categories of people who are comparable, at least to a certain extent, to the scientific experts of today.[14]

'Discovering the law' is precisely what my colleagues and I have been doing in various countries for the past fifteen years as a first step towards helping governments in developing countries build formal property systems that embrace all their people. When you push aside the Hollywood stereotypes of Third Worlders and ex-communists as a motley assortment of street vendors, mustachioed guerrillas and Slavic gangsters, you will find few differences between the cultures of the West and elsewhere when it comes to protecting assets and doing business. After years of study in many countries I have become convinced that most extralegal social contracts about property are basically similar to national social contracts in Western nations. Both tend to contain some explicit or tacit rules about who has rights over what and the limits to those rights and to transactions; they also include provisions to record ownership of assets, procedures to enforce property rights and claims, symbols to determine where the boundaries are, norms to govern transactions, criteria for deciding what requires authorized action and what can be carried out without authorization, guidelines to determine which representations are valid, devices to encourage people to honour contracts and respect the law, and criteria to determine the degree of anonymity authorized for each transaction.

It is fair to assume, therefore, that people are prepared to think about property rights in very similar ways. This should not come as a big surprise; folk conventions have always spread by analogy from one place to another spontaneously. Moreover, the massive migrations of the past forty years, not to mention the worldwide revolution in communications, mean that we are sharing more and more values and ambitions. (Third Worlders watch TV, too; they also go to the movies, use telephones and want their children to have good educations and become computer literate.) It is inevitable that individual extralegal social contracts in the same country will be more alike than different.[15]

The problem with extralegal social contracts is that their property representations are not sufficiently codified and fungible to have a broad range of application outside their own geographical parameters. Extralegal property systems are stable and meaningful for those who are part of the group, but they do operate at lower systemic levels and do not have representations that allow them to interact easily among each other. Again, this is similar to the past of the West when official titles did not exist. Before the fifteenth century in Europe, for example, even though some isolated registries did exist in some parts of what is today Germany, most official rules on how property transactions ought to work were unwritten and known only through oral traditions.

Many view those rituals and symbols as the representational predecessors of official titles, shares and records today. According to the eighteenth-century British philosopher and historian David Hume, in certain parts of Europe during his day landowners passed stones and earth between each other to commemorate the exchange of land; farmers symbolized the selling of wheat by handing over the key to the barn where it had been stored. Written parchments testifying to property transactions on land were ritually pressed to the soil to represent the agreement. Similarly, centuries before in Imperial Rome, Roman law provided that grass and branches were to be passed from hand to hand to represent the legal transfer of property rights. The Japanese, too, had their own ritual confirmations of transactions; for example, in the region of Gumma Kodzuke, during the Tokugawa period from the seventeenth to the nineteenth century when the sale of agricultural land was forbidden by law, land holders transferred their assets anyway, confirming these extralegal deals in written documents sealed by the seller's relatives and the village leader. Gradually, the written documents were collected in local registries. It took time before these representations were put in book form. But it was only during the nineteenth century that these different property registries and the social contracts governing them were standardized and brought together to create the integrated formal property systems that the West has today.

The former communist nations and the Third World are exactly where Europe, Japan and the United States were a couple of hundred years ago. Like the West, they must identify and gather up the existing property representations scattered throughout their nations and bring them into one integrated system to give the assets of all their citizens the fungibility, bureaucratic machinery and network required to produce capital.

Decoding Extralegal Law

When my colleagues and I first faced the task of integrating pre-capitalist property arrangements into a capitalist formal property system, the West was our inspiration. But when we started searching for the information on how the advanced nations integrated their extralegal arrangements into law, there were no blueprints for us to study. How Western nations identified which categories of extralegal proofs of property would be the common denominators of a standardized formal property system is unfortunately poorly documented. John Payne explains the situation in England:

> Formal proof of title as a part of commercial land transactions is apparently a late development in English law but present information is so scant as to make such a hypothesis merely tentative. It is a source of exasperation to the historian that,

while great events are chronicled in detail, people seldom feel it necessary to set down an account of the homely, everyday activities in which they engage. To do so would appear superfluous and banal, for no one wants to be reminded of the obvious. Consequently what everyone takes for granted in one era is unknown in the next, and the reconstruction of ordinary procedures requires painstaking piecing together of sources left for an altogether different purpose. This is certainly true of the practices of conveyancers, for, until the [nineteenth] century we have only limited knowledge of how they actually carried on their work.[16]

Guided by the few historical records we could find and filling the gaps with our own empirical research, we Brailled our way through extralegal worlds and eventually learned how to get in touch with the social contracts that underlay property rights there. Discovering these arrangements is nothing like searching for proofs of ownership in a formal legal system, where you can rely on a record-keeping system that has over the years created a paper trail, a 'chain of title', that allows you to search for its origin. In the undercapitalized sector, the chain of title is blurry, at best, to the outsider. The undercapitalized sector does not have, among other things, the centralized recording and tracking bureaucracy that is at the centre of formal society. What people in the undercapitalized sector do have are strong, clear and detailed understandings among themselves of who owns what today.

Consequently, the only way to find the extralegal social contract on property in a particular area is by contacting those who live and work by it. If property is like a tree, the formal the origins of each leaf back in time from twig and branch to the trunk and finally to the roots. The approach to extralegal property has to be synchronic: the only way an outsider can determine which rights belong to whom is by slicing the tree top at right angles to the trunk so as to define the status of each branch and leaf in relation to its neighbours.

Obtaining synchronic information takes fieldwork: going directly to those areas where property is not officially recorded (or poorly recorded) and getting in touch with local legal and extralegal authorities to find out what the property arrangements are. This is not as hard as it sounds. Although oral traditions may predominate in the rural backwoods of some countries, most people in the undercapitalized urban sector have found ways to represent their property in written form according to rules that they respect and that government, at some level, is forced to accept.

In Haiti, for instance, no one believed we would find documents fixing representations of property rights. Haiti is one of the world's poorest countries; 55 per cent of the population is illiterate. Nevertheless, after an intensive survey of Haiti's urban areas, we did not find a single extralegal plot of land, shack or building whose owner did not have at least one document to defend his right – even his 'squatting rights' (see Figure 6.2 for a selection of informal Haitian titles). Everywhere we have been in the world, most informals have some physical artefact to represent and substantiate their claim to property. And it is on the basis of these extralegal representations, as well as records and interviews, that we are everywhere able to extract the social contracts undergirding property.

While extralegal sources of information to identify property conventions are important, there are also official and legal sources. Politicians at the top are rarely conscious of the extent to which people at lower administrative levels of government are constantly in touch with the extralegal sector. Municipal authorities, urban planners, sanitation officers, police and many others have to produce official assessments of the extent of illegality of the informal settlements or groups of new businesses that are sprouting constantly throughout their districts. We have learned how to read official documentation to spot areas where extralegal social contracts prevail.

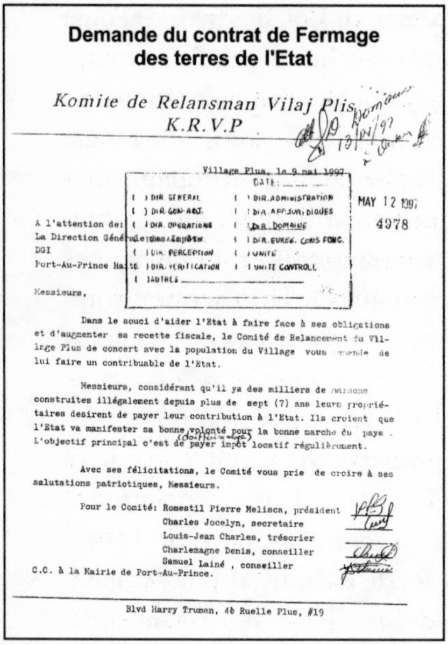

**Demande du contrat de Fermage
des terres de l'Etat**

Komite de Relansman Vilaj Plis
K.R.V.P

Village Plus, le 9 mai 1997

DATE:

( ) DIR GENERAL   ( ) DIR ADMINISTRATION
( ) DIR GEN ADJ   ( ) DIR AFF JURI DIQUES   MAY 12 1997
A l'attention de: ( ) DIR OPERATIONS   ( ) DIR DOMAINE   4978
La Direction Générale des Impôts ( ) DIR BUREG CONS FONC
DGI   ( ) DIR PERCEPTION   ( ) COMITE
Port-Au-Prince Haïti ( ) DIR VERIFICATION ( ) UNITE CONTROLL
                  ( ) AUTRES

Messieurs,

Dans le souci d'aider l'Etat à faire face à ses obligations et d'augmenter sa recette fiscale, le Comité de Relancement du Village Plus de concert avec la population du Village vous rende de lui faire un contribuable de l'Etat.

Messieurs, considérant qu'il y a des milliers de maisons construites illégalement depuis plus de sept (7) ans leurs propriétaires désirent de payer leur contribution à l'Etat. Ils croient que l'Etat va manifester sa bonne volonté pour la bonne marche du pays. L'objectif principal c'est de payer impôt locatif régulièrement.

Avec ses félicitations, le Comité vous prie de croire à ses salutations patriotiques, Messieurs.

Pour le Comité: Romestil Pierre Melisca, président
Charles Jocelyn, secrétaire
Louis-Jean Charles, trésorier
Charlemagne Denis, conseiller
Samuel Lainé, conseiller
C.C. à la Mairie de Port-au-Prince

Blvd Harry Truman, 4è Ruelle Plus, #19

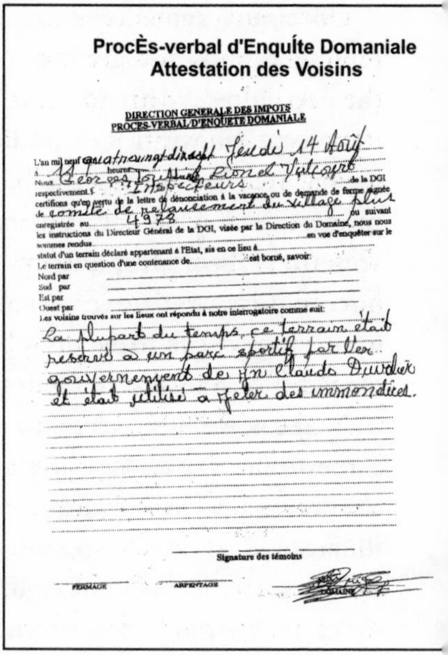

**ProcÈs-verbal d'Enquête Domaniale
Attestation des Voisins**

DIRECTION GENERALE DES IMPOTS
PROCÈS-VERBAL D'ENQUÊTE DOMANIALE

L'an mil neuf quatre-vingt-dix-sept Jeudi le 14 Août
Nous Gérard Joubert Lionel Vilaire
respectivement Inspecteurs de la DGI
certifions qu'en vertu de la lettre de dénonciation à la vacance, ou de demande de ferme signée de comité de relansement du Village Plus
enregistrée au   du suivant
les instructions du Directeur Général de la DGI, visée par la Direction du Domaine, nous nous sommes rendus   en vue d'enquêter sur le
statut d'un terrain déclaré appartenant à l'Etat, sis en ce lieu à
Le terrain en question d'une contenance de   est borné, savoir:
Nord par
Sud par
Est par
Ouest par
Les voisins trouvés sur les lieux ont répondu à notre interrogatoire comme suit:

La plupart du temps, ce terrain était réservé à un parc sportif par les gouvernements de Jn Claude Duvalier et était utilisé à jeter des immondices.

Signature des témoins

FERMAGE   ARPENTAGE

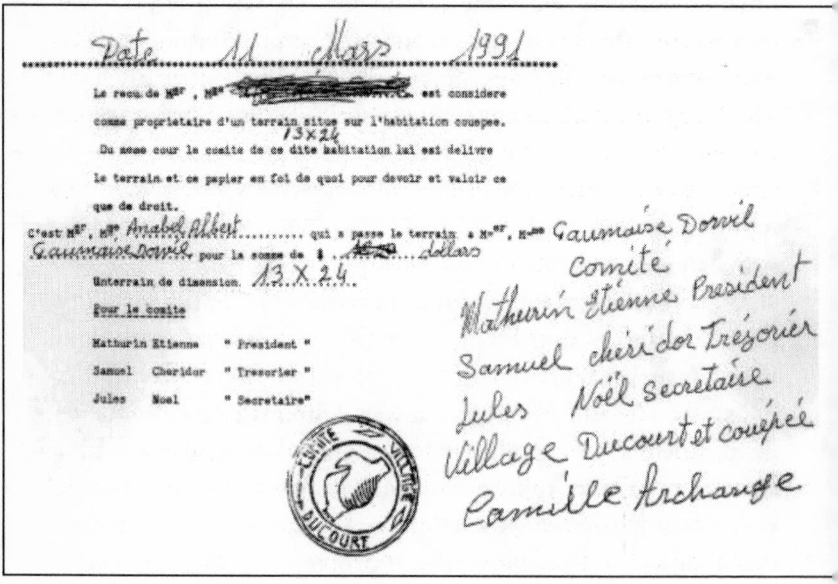

Date 11 Mars 1991

Le reçu de Mr, Mme   est considéré comme propriétaire d'un terrain situé sur l'habitation couepee.
13 X 24
Du même cœur le comité de ce dite habitation lui est délivre le terrain et ce papier en foi de quoi pour devoir et valoir ce que de droit.

C'est Mr, Mme Anabel Albert   qui a passé le terrain à Mr, Mme Gaumaise Dorvil
Gaumaise Dorvil pour la somme de $ dollars
Un terrain de dimension 13 X 24.

Pour le comité

Mathurin Etienne   " Président "
Samuel Cheridor   " Trésorier "
Jules Noël   " Secrétaire"

Comité
Mathurin Etienne Président
Samuel chéri'dor Trésorier
Jules Noël Secrétaire
Village Ducourt et couepée
Camille Archange

COMITE VILLAGE DUCOURT

**Figure 6.2
PROOFS OF OWNERSHIP USED BY INFORMALS IN HAITI**

Once governments know where to look for extralegal representations and get their hands on them, they have found the Ariadne's thread leading to the social contract. Representations are the result of a specific group of people having reached a respected consensus as to who owns what property and what each owner may do with it. Reading representations themselves and extracting meaning from them does not require a degree in archaeology. They contain no mysterious codes to be deciphered. People with very straightforward, businesslike intentions have written these documents to make absolutely clear to all concerned what rights they claim to have over the specific assets they control. They *want* to communicate the legitimacy of their rights and are prepared to provide as much supporting evidence as possible. Their representations have nothing to hide; they have been designed to be recognizable for what they are. This is not always so obvious because, regrettably, when dealing with the poor we tend to confuse the lack of a centralized record-keeping facility with ignorance. As John P. Powelson correctly concludes in *The Story of Land*, even in primitive rural areas of developing nations the people themselves have been their own most effective advocates and have always had the capacity to represent themselves intelligently.[17]

When governments obtain documentary evidence of representations, they can then 'deconstruct' them to identify the principles and rules that constitute the social contract that sustains them. Once reformers have done that, they will have all the major relevant pieces of extralegal law. The next task is to codify them – organize them in temporary formal statutes so that they can be examined and compared with existing formal law. Encoding loose systems is also not a problem; it is not much different from government procedures to make legal texts uniform within countries (such as the US Unified Commercial Code), or between countries at an international level (such as the many integrated mandatory codes produced by the European Union or the World Trade Organization). By comparing the extralegal to the legal codes, government leaders can see how both have to be adjusted to fit each other and then build a regulatory framework for property – a common bedrock of law for all citizens – that is genuinely legitimate and self-enforceable because it reflects both legal and extralegal reality. That is the way for developing and ex-communist nations to meet the legal challenge and was basically how Western law was built: by gradually discarding what was not useful and enforceable, and absorbing what worked.

If all this sounds more like an anthropological adventure than the basis for legal reform, it is because knowledge about the poor has been monopolized by academics, journalists and activists moved by compassion or intellectual curiosity rather than by the nuts and bolts of legal reform. Where have the lawyers been? Why haven't they taken a hard look at the law and order that their own people produce? The truth is that lawyers in these countries are generally too busy studying Western law and adapting it. They have been taught that local practices are not genuine law, but a romantic area of study best left to folklorists. But if lawyers want to play a role in creating good laws, they must step out of their law libraries into the extralegal sector, which is the only source of the information they need to build a truly legitimate formal legal system. By examining this 'people's law' and understanding its logic, reformers can get a sense of what they need to do to create a self-enforcing legal system.

When they have done this, governments will have literally touched the social contract. They will have the information required to integrate the poor and their possessions into a legal framework, so that they may finally begin to have a stake in the capitalist system. But implementing legal reform will mean tampering with the status quo. That makes it a major *political* task.

PART II:
The Political Challenge

Nobody planned the evolution from feudal and patrimonial systems to the modern property systems that exist in the West today. However, on the long evolutionary path to modernity, in those stretches of the journey when reformers embarked on deliberate programs to make property more accessible to a wider range of citizens, these programs were successful because they were supported by well-thought-out political strategies. That is what Thomas Jefferson did in Virginia at the end of the eighteenth century, when he increased the fungibility of property by abolishing, among other things, the practice of entail (not being able to transfer property outside the family). When Stein and Hardenberg set the stage for universal property rights in Germany at the beginning of the nineteenth century, and when Eugen Huber, in Switzerland at the beginning of the twentieth century, began to integrate all the dispersed property systems of his country, they likewise employed carefully planned strategies to storm the barricades of the status quo. They made sure that they were armed with astutely aimed legislation that permitted government to create popularly supported, bloodless revolutions that could not be halted.

Why do you need a political strategy today? Who could possibly be against removing so obviously unjust a legal apartheid? Few, in fact, would dispute the need for reform. But a tiny, powerful minority will intuit that reform is bound to perturb their little niches, and they will resist silently and insidiously. There is also a related problem: many of the statutes that wall off the majority of people from capital may also contain provisions that protect vital interests of powerful groups. Opening up capitalism to the poor will not be as simple as running a bulldozer through garbage. It is more like rearranging the thousands of branches and twigs of a huge eagle's nest –

without irritating the eagle. Although this rearrangement will impose only small inconveniences on this tiny minority, in comparison to the nationwide benefits of bringing capital to the poor, those affected will not see this unless reform is driven by a strong political initiative with the message and numbers to back it up.

Clearly, this is a job for experienced political operatives with the sophistication to rearrange the eagle's nest without being clawed. They are the only ones in a position to synchronize change for the majority and stability for the wary minorities. A strategy to capitalize the poor has to integrate two apparently contradictory property systems within the same body of law. If it is to succeed, a president or prime minister who is more than a mere technocrat has to take charge and make formalization a pillar of government policy. Only at the highest political level can reform command overwhelming support and wipe out the wilful inertia of the status quo. Only the top level of government can prevent bureaucratic infighting and political conflicts from paralysing the progress of reform. Whenever a nation sets out to make a major change, whether to stabilize money, privatize government agencies or open up the schools to all races, the head of state steps forward to lead the charge. Emancipating the poor surely falls within the responsibilities of the nation's leader.

History and personal experience have taught us that, to make a property revolution, a leader has to do at least three specific things: take the perspective of the poor, co-opt the élite and deal with the legal and technical bureaucracies that are the bell jar's current custodians.

Taking the Perspective of the Poor

Everyone will benefit from globalizing capitalism within a country, but the most obvious and largest beneficiary will be the poor. With the poor on his side, a leader intent on reform has already won at least half the battle. Any opposition will be hard pressed to take on the head of state and most of the people. But, to win, he or she will have to acquire the facts necessary to build a case. This involves carrying out original research: reformers have to put themselves in the shoes of the poor and walk their streets. Official statistics do not contain the information they need. The facts and figures can only be seen from outside the bell jar.

When I began studying the possibility of giving the poor access to formal property in Peru in the 1980s, every major law firm I consulted assured me that setting up a formal business to access capital would take only a few days. I knew this was true for me and my lawyers, but I had a hunch it was not true for the majority of Peruvians. So my colleagues and I decided to set up a two-sewing-machine garment factory in a Lima shanty town. To experience the process from the point of view of the poor, we used a stopwatch to measure the amount of time a typical entrepreneur in Lima would have to spend to get through the red tape. We discovered that to become legal took over three hundred days, working six hours a day. The cost: thirty-two times the monthly minimum wage. We performed a similar experiment to find out what it would take for a person living in an extralegal housing settlement, whose permanence the government had already acknowledged, to acquire legal title to a home. To receive approval from only the municipality of Lima – just one of the eleven governmental agencies involved – took 728 bureaucratic steps (see Figure 6.3). This confirmed what I suspected from the beginning: most conventional data reflects the interests of those, like the lawyers I consulted, who are already inside the bell jar. That is why the bell jar can be seen only from the outside looking in: from the perspective of the poor.

Once government obtains this information, it will be able to explain its intent in a way the poor can understand and relate to. As a result, they will support the agenda of reform enthusiastically. The poor will become the most effective public

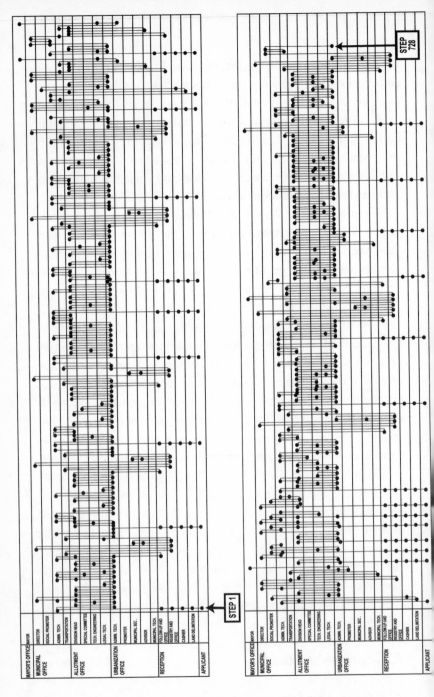

Figure 6.3
**728 BUREAUCRATIC STEPS REQUIRED BY THE MUNICIPALITY
OF LIMA TO OBTAIN LEGAL TITLE TO A HOME IN A
VALIDATED HOUSING SETTLEMENT**

relations machine for reform, providing the feedback from the streets necessary to keep the program on course.

This is what happened in Peru. From 1984 to 1994 my colleagues and I directed all our efforts to informing the public about the benefits of lifting the bell jar (at the time we called it 'formalization'). Our objective was to prove to the politicians that there was a hidden national consensus for reform and that formalizing the assets of the poor was politically a winning strategy. By the late 1980s the polls confirmed this: our proposals to change the formal property system had an approval rating of nearly 90 per cent. With numbers like that, it was not surprising that when the first pieces of legislation and regulations that my organization drafted for formalization came before the Peruvian Congress in 1988 and early 1990, they were unanimously approved. During the 1990 presidential campaign every candidate, including Mario Vargas Llosa, the novelist and candidate of the libertarian–conservative coalition, and Alberto Fujimori, the dark-horse populist and eventual winner, along with the outgoing socialist president Alan Garcia, subscribed to the agenda of formalization. Even today, in spite of implementation efforts that have been erratic and very incomplete, formalization is an uncontested and permanent fixture on the Peruvian political landscape.

With the facts, figures and public opinion all on the side of reform, the government will be in a position to move the whole issue of poverty dramatically into its agenda for economic growth. Relieving poverty will no longer be seen as a charitable cause, to be undertaken if and when it ever becomes affordable. On the contrary, the future of the poor can now top the list of the government's program for growth.

Co-opting the Elites

Once the economic potential of the poor – the largest constituency in the nation – has been revealed and their support for reform is manifest, reformers will have the attention of the élite. This is the moment to break their illusion that lifting the bell jar benefits only the poor. It is not only that bridging the gap between classes is a general social good. This kind of legal integration can help almost every interest group in the nation. Just as reformers collected facts and numbers to win the support of the poor, they must use other facts and figures to win over vested interests. The élites must support reform not out of patriotism or altruism but because it will also enlarge their wallets.

For example, bringing the extralegal sector inside the law will open up the opportunity for massive low-cost housing programs that will provide the poor with homes that are not only better built but much cheaper than what they themselves have been building in the extralegal sector. Creating a home in the topsy-turvy world of the extralegal sector is equivalent to getting dressed by putting on your shoes first, then your socks. Consider what it takes for a new migrant from a rural area to create a home for his family in a shanty town outside a large city. First, he not only has to find a spot for his house, but has to occupy the land *personally*, with his family. The next step is to set up a tent or shelter made from, depending on the country, straw matting, mud bricks, cardboard, plywood, corrugated iron or tin cans – and thus stake out a physical claim (because a legal one is unavailable). The migrant and his family will then gradually bring in furniture and other house-hold items. Obviously, they need a more livable and durable edifice. But how to build it without access to credit? They do what everyone else does – stock solid building materials and begin to build a better house, stage by stage, according to what kinds of material they can accumulate.

Once the inhabitants of one of these new neighbourhoods have organized enough to protect their holdings or the local authorities take pity on their deprivation, they can bring in pavement, water, waste-disposal and electricity – typically at the cost of having to destroy parts of their houses in order to hook up to the utilities. Only after years of building and rebuilding, and saving construction materials, are these home-owners finally in a position to live comfortably.

In the West creating a home is the equivalent of putting on your socks before your shoes, and is thus much less hazardous, expensive and degrading. A developer typically holds title to the land which gives him the security to develop the infra-structure (paved roads, utilities, etc.). Then he sells the house, which he proceeds to build according to the buyer's prefer-ences. The new owners, who have probably borrowed most of the price of the house from a bank, will then move their furniture in and, finally, the kids and the cat.

At the moment when the poor become accountable under formal law they will be able to afford low-cost housing and thus escape from the topsy-turvy world of the extralegal sector. The élites will then begin to collect their rewards as well: builders and construction material manufacturers will find their markets expanding, as will banks, mortgage companies, title agencies and insurance firms. Formalization will also help the suppliers of public utilities to convert home addresses into liable terminals. It will provide governments and businesses with information and addresses for merchandising, securing interests and collecting debts, fees and taxes. In addition a formal property system supplies a database for investment decisions in healthcare, education, tax assessment and environmental planning.

Widespread legal property will even help solve one of their loudest and most persistent complaints about the expanding urban poor —the need for more 'law and order'. Civil society in market economies is not simply due to greater prosperity. The right to property also engenders respect for law. As the eminent historian Richard Pipes pointed out in his book about the Russian Revolution:

> Private property is arguably the single most important institution of social and political integration. Ownership of

property creates a commitment to the political and legal order since the latter guarantees property rights: it makes the citizen into a co-sovereign, as it were. As such, property is the principal vehicle for inculcating in the mass of the population respect for law and an interest in the preservation of the status quo. Historical evidence indicates that societies with a wide distribution of property, notably in land and residential housing, are more conservative and stabler, and for that reason more resilient to upheavals of all sorts. Thus the French peasant, who in the eighteenth century was a source of instability, became in the nineteenth, as a result of the gains of the French Revolution, a pillar of conservatism.[18]

When poor people have confidence that their land and businesses are legally theirs, their respect for other people's property increases.

Formal, up-to-date property records will also provide the police with the information necessary for civilized restraint. In developing and former communist nations one of the chief characteristics of outlaws is not having a legal address. When a crime is committed, police do not have the records, leads and other property-based information necessary to 'skip trace' prime suspects. That is why law enforcement authorities cannot be as selective as their Western counterparts when rounding up suspects and are thus more likely to violate people's civil rights.

Owning formal property also tends to discourage unruly behaviour. When people are forced to divide their property into smaller and smaller parcels, the heirs of their heirs, crowded off the family land, are more likely to squat elsewhere. Also, when a person cannot prove he owns anything he is more likely to have to bribe his way through the bureaucracy, or with the help of his neighbours, take the law into his own hands. Worse still, without good law to enforce obligations, society in effect invites the gangsters and terrorists to do the job. My colleagues and I have carried out formal titling campaigns that have displaced terrorists by co-opting their role as the area's security force against the real or imagined threat of land expropriation.

Property also provides a legal alternative to drug trafficking. As long as the farmers remain illegal landowners, short-term cash crops, like coca and opium poppies, remain their only alternative. For small farmers in some areas of the developing world, money advanced by drug traffickers is practically the only credit available, and because their property arrangements appear in no official system, law enforcement cannot even find them, never mind work out an enforceable crop-substitution agreement. This lack of legal protection also means that growers of drug crops have to band together to defend their assets or call on traffickers to defend them. Without a formal property system that includes such landowners, controlling growers of drug crops, chasing drug traffickers and identifying environment polluters becomes virtually impossible. There is no way for authorities to penetrate the tight extralegal arrangements the people create to protect their interests.

Legalizing property is hardly mere charity for the poor. Creating an orderly market that makes owners accountable and gives their homes clear titles worthy of financing will generate an expanded market, encourage law and order and put money into the pockets of the élite.

Dealing with the Custodians of the Bell Jar

Once reformers have the poor and at least some of the élite on their side, it will be time to take on the public and private bureaucracy who administer and maintain the status quo – principally, the lawyers and the technicians.

The Lawyers

In theory the legal community should favour reform because it will expand the rule of law. But most lawyers in developing and former communist countries have been trained not to expand the rule of law but to defend it as they found it. Lawyers are the professionals most involved in the day-to-day business of property. They sit in the key government offices where they exert a stranglehold on major decisions. No group – aside from terrorists – is better positioned to sabotage capitalist expansion. And, unlike terrorists, the lawyers know how to do it legally.

Although entrepreneurs and ordinary people are the builders of capital and capitalism, it is the lawyers who fix property concepts in tangible representative form and define those concepts in statutes. The security of ownership, the accountability of owners and the enforceability of transactions must ultimately be concretized in procedures and rules drafted by lawyers. It is the legal profession that perfects all the artefacts of formal property: titles, records, trademarks, copyrights, promissory notes, bills of exchange, patent rights, shares of corporate stock. Whether you like lawyers or not, no genuine change in the property regime and the capital formation process will take place without the cooperation of at least some of them.

The difficulty is that few lawyers understand the economic consequences of their work, and their knee-jerk reaction to extralegal behaviour and to large-scale change is generally hostile. All the reformers I have met working to make property more accessible to the poor operate with the presumption that the legal profession is their natural enemy. Economists involved in reform have become so frustrated with legal conservatism that they have invested time and money to discredit the legal profession. Using economic data from fifty-two countries from 1960 to 1980, Samar K. Datta and Jeffrey B. Nugent have shown that for every percentage point increase in the number of lawyers in the labour force (from, say, 0.5 to 1.5 per cent), economic growth is reduced by 4.76 to 3.68 per cent – thus showing that economic growth is inversely related to the prudence of lawyers.[19]

What especially irritates many reformers is how lawyers shift the blame for bad property systems to other people. I have often heard lawyers commending existing property law, while in the same breath conceding that legally issued property titles were difficult or impossible to use. This is, of course, unacceptable. A lawyer cannot design the law and the administrative procedures for implementing it and then blame its failure on the inadequacies of the low-level technocrats who implement the law or the poor education of those who use it. It is not enough to draft elegant laws. They must also work in the administrative and social reality for which they were drafted.

Interestingly, the strongest criticism of lawyers' efforts to stall property reform often comes from their fellow-attorneys. S. Rowton Simpson, a lawyer and the world's most renowned author on the subject of land registration, writes of his colleagues:

Lawyers, the world over, are notorious for their reluctance to accept even the smallest changes in their traditional procedures . . . Torrens [the Australian creator of one of the world's most secure recording systems], who was opposed tooth and nail by the legal profession, overcame the opposition of the lawyers in South Australia; but his story is exceptional. It takes a diamond to cut a diamond, and in most countries registration of title has, as a rule, owed its introduction to the efforts of a lawyer, handicapped as he may have been by the active opposition of the practising members of his profession; and passive opposition may be even worse than active, which at least either wins or is defeated. Passive opposition is more insidious; it can stultify progress. Not a few statutes have withered on the vine after receiving a welcome from practitioners which proved to be merely lip service or even 'the kiss of death'; other statutes have had built into them a procedure so long-term as to make progress almost imperceptible; such statutes certainly offer no dangers to established practice, and so tend to be acceptable to the legal profession, but they do not really achieve the objective; they merely swell the list, if not of failures, at least of 'non-successes'.[20]

Although lawyers often concede that other disciplines have to be dynamic, they argue that the law must be stable. Such veneration of the rule of law, no matter the consequences, can reach the point where attorneys who support reform risk ostracism by their peers. In German-speaking countries during the nineteenth and early twentieth centuries the legal profession's hostility towards property reform ran so high that any reformist lawyer was called a *Mestbeschmutzer* – a beast that fouls its own nest.

The good news for reformers is that the most brilliant (but not necessarily the most successful) lawyers believe that law is made to serve life and not the other way around. Forward-looking jurists ultimately triumphed over the reactionary tendency of their profession in the West, even in the context of Roman law. To be sure, the battle was uphill all the way, mainly because, as Peter Stein has remarked, lawyers' 'contribution to a proper understanding of legal institutions was obscured by their emphasis on antiquarianism and their acceptance of Roman law as a finished product'.[21] Nevertheless, over time, great European jurists overcame excessive rigidity because, as Stein points out, they 'made it their profession to become experts in the intricacies of the Roman law, and to ensure that it moved with the time'.[22] Against their colleagues' rampant unresponsiveness, in every European country an élite band of lawyers emerged to help lift the bell jar.

Any government eager to pursue an integrated property system must therefore draw up a careful strategy for dealing with the legal profession. The key is choosing the right lawyers. It takes a wise and cunning political leader to avoid the lawyers skilled at the subtleties of scaring politicians into a state of immobility and to find instead those who will give legal form to an agenda for transformation even if it means bucking the system. Unless the reform-minded politician hand-picks his lawyers, he will be at the mercy of the ruling legal technocrats who will give lip service to reform while subverting it in the shadows.

Courageous, reform-minded lawyers exist in every nation, and once the selection criteria for such qualities is clear, the right people can be identified. Many understand that the primary determinants of change rest outside the law. In every country I have visited I have found groups of government lawyers very familiar with the extralegal sector, striving daily to find harmony between the formal system and the extralegal arrangements. Some academic lawyers are also acutely aware that the parallel orders of legal and extralegal law operate simultaneously. But their work tends to go unnoticed in the higher reaches of government, and so they, too, remain invisible. Indeed, it is nearly a rule that lawyers who are clued in to the existence of the two orders and are sympathetic with reform are pushed to the margins of political decision-making.

It is these people whom the political leadership must marshal to storm the status quo and implement an irresistible national programme to formalize property. Such an army, however, does not step forward spontaneously. Each lawyer must be located and recruited. Altogether, they will form the vanguard that can make the case of reform to their fellow-lawyers. It is they who will be able to beat back the dinosaurs and explain to the legal profession in its own language how crucial it is to their own and their nation's future to integrate all property into one unified legal system open to all people. They alone can explain to the rest of the profession that existing legal procedures have become not simply a nuisance but *the* insurmountable obstacle that keeps most of the people of the world from being in a position to create capital.

Lawyers are human, too. Once they understand that the system they defend is hopelessly outdated, they will react positively.

The Technicians

Developing and former communist countries are forever spending hundreds of millions of dollars on mapping and computerized record-keeping technology to modernize their property systems —and they still cannot integrate their extralegal sectors. This no longer surprises anyone who has thought hard about the priorities of property reform. In 1993 a World Bank expert warned that 'There has been a tendency to consider land titling a technical problem. Often the maps are made and surveys carried out, but the titles are not made or issued because of a blockage in systems or legal problems.'[23]

Even the technicians are concerned that they may be too mesmerized by the amazing new technologies. One of Canada's foremost experts in land and information systems has expressed concern that some governments continue to view mapping as the cornerstone of property:

> We are currently in danger of perpetuating this myth by trying to reduce resource management to a geographical information system (GIS) problem. Technology is attractive; it produces tangible results. But it is only part of the solution ... Consultants and aid organizations frequently export systems they are familiar with (usually their own or ones they have worked with) without giving sufficient consideration to the needs and constraints of the recipient country ... There is a need for more modesty among professional consultants; there is a need to occasionally admit that they do not always know the answer or that their system may not be appropriate.[24]

Property creation programmes will continue to fail as long as governments think that creating property only requires getting acquainted with physical things – that once they have photo-graphed, surveyed, measured and computerized the inventories of their physical assets they have all the information required to issue property titles. They do not. Photographs and inventories only inform authorities of the physical state of the assets; they say nothing about who really owns those assets or how people have organized the rights that govern them. All the photographs and computer inventories in the world cannot tell anyone what local rules enforce these rights or what network of relationships sustains them. As important as maps and inventories are to measure and locate the physical assets to which property is anchored, they do not tell governments how to build the national social contract that will enable them to create widespread legal property.

The propensity in some countries to squeeze the issues related to property into the departments of mapping and information technology has obscured the real nature of property. Property is not really part of the physical world: its natural habitat is legal and economic. Property is about invisible things, while maps are resemblances of physical things on the ground. Maps capture the physical information of assets but miss the big picture. Without the pertinent institutional and economic information about extralegal arrangements they cannot capture the reality outside the bell jar. They are thus unable to do their real job, which is to help anchor the property aspects of assets in physical reality so as to keep virtuality and physicality in sync.

Until the obstacles to using formal property systems are removed and the extralegal arrangements have been replaced by the law, people have little incentive to supply the information necessary to keep maps and data bases updated and reliable. People do not want to get inside the formal property system because they are eager to be mapped, recorded or taxed; they will join the system when its economic benefits are obvious to them and when they are certain their rights will continue to be protected.

As long as these rights are protected by an extralegal social contract, people will see no reason to notify authorities of any changes in the disposition of their assets. Only when formal law replaces extralegal arrangements as the source of protection for property will people accept its legitimacy and be interested in providing authorities with the information required to keep their maps and records current. The place where the social contract is located determines where the records and maps can be kept current.

This is not a trivial point. Technically driven titling projects tend to degenerate into identification systems for physical stock, outdated Domesday Books or historical relics. The mapping and computer industries suffer as a result. Their project budgets are approved by politicians who expect that these new methods will incorporate the poor. Once they realize they do not, the mapping projects get scaled down or terminated. My team and I have found this happening time and again.

These technologies work so well in advanced nations, without the need for much legal and political tinkering, because the tinkering was done more than a hundred years ago. The all-encompassing social contract on property is already firmly in place. When the database systems, geographical information systems, remote sensing, global positioning system, and all the wonderful information technology tools became available during the last thirty years, they could fit neatly into a well-integrated information and legal infrastructure. Thus the written and graphic representational devices, and facilities for better storage, retrieval and manipulation of information, could be put to good use.

I am not saying that engineering, systems integration, information technology companies, equipment vendors, registry advisers and all the others who provide property documentation services specialized in surveying, mapping and the modernization of registries are unimportant to property creation – quite the contrary. If appropriately adapted to massive registration and to operating in an extralegal environment, they are indispensable for defining physical locations as well as for processing and integrating information. They will consume most of the money spent on property reform, but only after the legal and political problems of bringing in the extralegal sector are solved.

Only true political leadership can coax the law of property out of its preoccupation with the past and into an appreciation of the present; from being much too impressed with technology to becoming concerned with the good of society. Politicians are needed because existing institutions are inclined to favour and protect the status quo. It is a political task to persuade technocracy to make itself over and support change.

Political intervention is also necessary because government organizations within the bell jar are generally not designed to undertake swift, broad reform programs. They are usually organized as specialized departments, a structure that makes more sense in developed nations, where only gradual change is necessary because the law and formal property are already functioning for all. Property creation is not at all like a privatization programme, which only involves selling a dozen or so bundles of assets a year. The goal of property reform is to award property rights for millions of assets to millions of people in a short time. This means that at least half the job is about communications. The leaders of property reform need to describe how popular capitalism will affect many different interest groups, show them the benefits they will derive from it and persuade them that it is a win–win exercise for all segments of society. For the extralegal sector, these leaders must address their pent-up entrepreneurial energy and demonstrate the advantages of integrating a new formal law. For the legal sector, they must explain that the proposed reforms will not hurt legitimate and enforceable rights and that there will be aggregate gains for all interest groups.

Creating a property system that is accessible to all is

primarily a political job because it has to be kept on track by people who understand that the final goal of a property system is not drafting elegant statutes, connecting shiny computers or printing multicoloured maps but putting capital in the hands of the whole nation.

7

By Way of Conclusion

Where is the wisdom we have lost in knowledge?
Where is the knowledge we have lost in information?
T.S. ELIOT, Choruses from 'The Rock'

The Private Club of Globalization

Capitalism is in crisis outside the West not because international globalization is failing but because developing and ex-communist nations have been unable to 'globalize' capital within their own countries. Most people in those nations view capitalism as a private club, a discriminatory system that benefits only the West and the élites who live inside the bell jars of poor countries.

More people throughout the world may wear Nike shoes and flash their digital watches, but even as they consume the goods of the West, they are quite aware that they still linger at the periphery of the capitalist game. They have no stake in it. Globalization should not be just about interconnecting the bell jars of the privileged few. That kind of globalization has existed before: in the nineteenth century Europe's ruling royals were literally one big family, related by blood and in constant contact about politics and commerce with their cousins in

England, France, Holland, Spain and Russia. Capitalism triumphed in the nineteenth century and prevailed throughout the industrialized world until the Russian Revolution and the Great Depression. But as Spain's Ortega y Gasset and the American pundit Walter Lippman pointed out, despite its dominance and sophistication, the capitalist system was always vulnerable. The American economist Lester Thurow points out that as recently as 1941:

> the United States and Great Britain were essentially the only [major] capitalist countries left on the face of the earth . . . All the rest of the world were fascists, communists or Third World feudal colonies. The final crisis of the 1920s and the Great Depression of the 1930s had brought capitalism to the edge of extinction. The capitalism that now seems irresistible could, with just a few missteps, have vanished.[1]

Latin Americans do not have to be reminded. On at least four occasions since their independence from Spain in the 1820s they have tried to become part of global capitalism and failed. They restructured their debts, stabilized their economies by controlling inflation, liberalized trade, privatized government assets (selling their railroads to the British, for example), undertook debt equity swaps and overhauled their tax systems. At the consumer level, the Latin Americans imported all sorts of goods, from English tweed suits and Church shoes to Model T Fords; they learned English and French by listening to the radio or records; they danced the Charleston and the Lambeth Walk, and chewed Chiclets gum. But they never produced much live capital.

We may now all be benefiting from the communications revolution, and some may see progress in the fact that the Egyptian Sphinx now stares directly at the neon sign of a Kentucky Fried Chicken franchise. Nevertheless, only twenty-five of the world's two hundred countries produce capital in sufficient quantity to benefit fully from the division of labour in expanded global markets. The lifeblood of capitalism is not the Internet or fast-food franchises. It is *capital*. Only capital provides the means to support specialization and the production and exchange of assets in the expanded market. It is capital that is the source of increasing productivity and therefore the wealth of nations.

Yet only the Western nations and small enclaves of wealthy people in developing and former communist nations have the capacity to represent assets and potential, and, therefore, the ability to produce and use capital efficiently. Capitalism is viewed outside the West with increasing hostility, as an apartheid regime most cannot enter. There is a growing sense, even among some élites, that if they have to depend solely and for ever on the kindness of outside capital, they will never be productive players in the global capitalist game. They are increasingly frustrated at not being masters of their own fates. Since they have embarked on globalization without providing their own people with the means to produce capital, they are beginning to look less like the United States than like mercantilist Latin America with its disarray of extralegal activity.[2] Ten years ago few would have compared the former Soviet bloc nations to Latin America. But today they look astonishingly similar: strong underground economies, glaring inequality, pervasive mafias, political instability, capital flight and flagrant disregard for law.

That is why outside the West advocates of capitalism are intellectually on the retreat. Ascendant just a decade ago, they are now increasingly viewed as apologists for the miseries and injustices that still affect the majority of people. For example, in 1999 Egypt's consultative upper house warned the government 'not to be deceived any longer by calls for capitalism and globalization'.[3] Having forgotten the crucial issue of property, capitalism's advocates have let themselves become identified as the defenders of the status quo, blindly trying to enforce existing written law whether it discriminates or not.

And the law in those countries does discriminate. As I

illustrated in Chapter 2, at least 80 per cent of the population in these countries cannot inject life into their assets and make them generate capital because the law keeps them out of the formal property system. They have trillions of dollars in dead capital, but it is as if these were isolated ponds whose waters disappear into a sterile strip of sand, instead of forming a mighty mass of water that can be captured in one unified property system and given the form required to produce capital. People hold and use their assets on the basis of myriad disconnected informal agreements where accountability is managed locally. Without the common standards that legal property brings, they lack the language necessary for their assets to talk to each other. There is no use urging them to be patient until the benefits of capitalism trickle down their way. That will never happen until the firm foundations of formal property are in place.

Meanwhile, the promoters of capitalism, still arrogant and drunk on their victory over communism, have yet to understand that their macroeconomic reforms are not enough. We must not forget that globalization is occurring because developing and former communist nations are opening up their once protected economies, stabilizing their currencies and drafting regulatory frameworks to enhance international trade and private investment. All of this is good. What is not so good is that these reforms assume that these countries' populations are already integrated into the legal system and have the same ability to use their resources in the open market. They do not.

As I have argued in Chapter 3, most people cannot participate in an expanded market because they do not have access to a legal property rights system that represents their assets in a manner that makes them widely transferable and fungible, that allows them to be encumbered and permits their owners to be held accountable. So long as the assets of the majority are not properly documented and tracked by a property bureaucracy, they are invisible and sterile in the market place.

By stabilizing and adjusting by 'the book', the globalizers' macroeconomic programmes have dramatically rationalized the economic management of developing countries. But because their book does not address the fact that most people do not have property rights, they have done only a fraction of the work required to create a comprehensive capitalist system and market economy. Their tools are designed to work in countries where systematized law has been 'globalized' internally, when inclusive property rights systems that link up to efficient monetary and investment instruments are in place – something these countries have yet to develop.

Too many policy-makers have taken an Olympian view of the globalization process. Once they stabilized and adjusted at the macro level, allowing legal business and foreign investors to prosper and orthodox economists to control the treasury, they felt they had fulfilled their duty. Because they concentrated only on policies dealing with the aggregates, they did not have to enquire if people had the means to participate in an expanded market system. They forgot that people are the fundamental agents of change and they forgot to focus on the poor. And they made that enormous omission because they do not operate while keeping the concept of *class* in mind. In the words of one of their most outstanding pundits, they do not have 'the ability to comprehend, however dimly, how other people live'.[4]

Economic reformers have left the issue of property for the poor in the hands of conservative legal establishments uninterested in changing the status quo. As a result, the assets of the majority of their citizens have remained dead capital stuck in the extralegal sector. This is why the advocates of globalization and free market reforms are beginning to be perceived as the self-satisfied defenders of the interests of those who dominate the bell jar.

Facing up to Marx's Ghost

Most economic reform programmes in poor economies may be falling into the trap that Karl Marx foresaw: the great contradiction of the capitalist system is that it creates its own demise because it cannot avoid concentrating capital in a few hands. By not giving the majority access to expanded markets, these reforms are leaving a fertile field for class confrontation – a capitalist and free market economy for the privileged few who can concretize their property rights, and relative poverty for a large undercapitalized sector incapable of leveraging its own assets.

Class confrontations, in this day and age? Didn't that concept come down with the Berlin Wall? Unfortunately, it did not. This may be hard for a citizen in an advanced nation to understand because in the West those discontented with the system live in 'pockets of poverty'.[5] Misery in developing and ex-communist nations, however, is not contained in pockets; it is spread throughout society. What few pockets exist in those countries are pockets of wealth. What the West calls 'the underclass' is here the majority. And in the past, when their rising expectations were not met, that mass of angry poor brought apparently solid élites to their knees (as in Iran, Venezuela and Indonesia). In most countries outside the West governments depend on strong intelligence services and their elites live behind fortress-like walls for good reason.

Today, to a great extent, the difference between advanced nations and the rest of the world is that between countries where formal property is widespread and countries where classes are divided into those who can fix property rights and produce capital and those who cannot. If extralegal property rights are not accommodated, these societies may muddle along with their dual economies – with the so-called law-abiding sector on one side and the impoverished extralegal sector on the other. But as information and communications continue to improve and the poor become better informed of what they do not have, the bitterness over legal apartheid is bound to grow. At some point those outside the bell jar will be mobilized against the status quo by people with political agendas that thrive on discontent. 'If we do not invent ways to make globalization more inclusive,' says Klaus Schwab of the World Economic Forum, 'we have to face the prospect of a resurgence of the acute social confrontations of the past, magnified at the international level.'[5]

The Cold War may have ended, but the old class arguments have not disappeared. Subversive activities and an upsurge of ethnic and cultural conflicts around the world prove that when people are extremely dissatisfied they continue to constitute themselves into classes based on shared injuries. *Newsweek* notes that in the Americas since the 1980s, 'each of these struggles has its own unique history, but the fighters all vilify the same enemy: the new face of Latin American capitalism.'[6] In such situations the Marxist toolkit is better geared to explain class conflict than capitalist thinking, which has no comparable analysis or even a serious strategy for reaching the poor in the extralegal sector. Capitalists generally have no systemic explanation of how the people in the underclass got where they are and how the system could be changed to raise them up.

We must not underestimate the latent power of Marxist integrated theory at a time when masses of people with little hope are looking for a cohesive worldview to improve their desperate economic prospects. In a period of economic boom, there tends to be little time for deep thinking. Crisis, however, has a way of sharpening the mind's need for order and explanations into obsession. Marxist thinking, in whatever form it reappears – and it will – supplies a much mightier array of concepts for grappling with the political problems of capitalism outside the West than capitalist thinking does.

Marx's insights into capital, as George Soros recently observed, are often more sophisticated than those of Adam Smith.[7] Marx understood clearly that 'in themselves money and commodities are no more capital than are the means of productions and of subsistence. That they want transforming into capital.'[8] He also understood that if assets could be converted into commodities and made to interact in markets, they could express values that are imperceptible to the senses but can be captured to produce rents. For Marx, property was an important issue because it was clear to him that those who appropriated the assets obtained much more than just their physical attributes. As a result, the Marxist intellectual toolkit has left anti-capitalists powerful ways to explain why private property will necessarily put assets in the hands of the rich at the expense of the poor.

For those who have not noticed, the arsenal of anti-capitalism and anti-globalization is building up. Today there are serious statistics that provide the anti-capitalists with just the ammunition they need to argue that capitalism is a transfer of property from poorer to richer countries; that Western private investment in developing nations is nothing short of a massive takeover of their resources by multinationals. The number of flashy cars, luxurious homes and California-style shopping malls may have increased in most developing and ex-communist nations over the past decade, but so have the poor. Nancy Birdsall and Juan Luis Londoño's research shows that poverty has grown faster and income distribution has worsened over the last decade.[9] According to a 1999 United Nations 'Human Development Report,' gross domestic product in the Russian Federation fell by 41 percent from 1990 to 1997, driving millions into the extralegal sector. The life expectancy of the Russian male has dropped four full years – to fifty-eight. The report blames the transition to capitalism and the effects of globalization.

These research efforts provide us with healthy warning signals, but they are also putting in place the intellectual missiles needed to discourage privatization programmes and global capitalism. It is crucial, therefore, to recognize the latent Marxist paradigms and then add what we have learned in the century since Marx died. We can now demonstrate that though Marx clearly saw that a parallel economic life can be generated alongside physical assets themselves – that 'the productions of the human brain appeared as independent beings endowed with life'[10] – he did not quite grasp that formal property was not simply an instrument for appropriation but also the means to motivate people to create real additional usable value. Moreover, he did not see that it is the mechanisms contained in the property system itself that give assets and the labour invested in them the form required to create capital. Although Marx's analysis of how assets become transcendent and serve greater social uses when they become exchangeable is fundamental to understanding wealth, he was not able to foresee to what degree legal property systems would become crucial vehicles for the enhancement of exchange value.

Marx understood, better than anyone else in his time, that in economics there is no greater blindness than seeing resources exclusively in terms of their physical properties. He was well aware that capital was 'an independent substance . . . in which money and commodities are mere forms which it assumes and casts off in turn'.[11] But he lived in a time when it was probably still too soon to see how formal property could, through representation, make those same resources serve additional functions and produce surplus value. Consequently, Marx could not see how it would be in everyone's interest to increase the range of the beneficiaries of property. Property titles were only the visible tip of a growing formal property iceberg. The rest of the iceberg is now an enormous man-made facility for drawing out the economic potential of assets. That is why Marx did not fully understand that legal property is the indispensable process that fixes and deploys capital; that without property mankind cannot convert the fruits of its labour into fungible, liquid forms that can be differentiated, combined, divided and invested to produce surplus value. He did not realize that a good legal property system, like a Swiss army knife, has many more mechanisms than just the elementary 'ownership' blade.

Much of Marx's thought is outdated because the situation today is not the same as in Marx's Europe. Potential capital is no longer the privilege of the few. After Marx's death, the West finally managed to set up a legal framework that gave most people access to property and the tools of production. Marx would probably be shocked to find how in developing countries much of the teeming mass does not consist of oppressed legal proletarians but of oppressed extralegal small entrepreneurs with a sizeable amount of assets.

Admiration for good property systems should not blind us to the fact that, as Marx noted, these systems can also be used for theft. The world will always be full of sharks expert at using property paper to skim off wealth from unsuspecting people. Yet one cannot oppose formal property systems for this reason, any more than one should abolish computers or automobiles because people use them to commit crimes. If Marx were alive today and saw the misappropriation of resources that has occurred on both sides of the former Iron Curtain, he would probably agree that looting can happen with or without property, and that controlling thievery depends more on the exercise of power than on property. In addition, though Marx gave 'surplus value' a very specific definition, its meaning is not chained to his pen. People have always produced surplus value to create pyramids, cathedrals, expensive armies, to name a few examples. Clearly much of today's surplus value in the West has originated not in scandalously expropriated labour time but in the way that property has given minds the mechanisms with which to extract additional work from commodities.

Like all of us, Marx was influenced by the social conditions and technologies of his time. The expropriation of small pro-prietors from their means of subsistence, the access to private property rights stemming from feudal title, the robbery of common lands, the enslavement of aboriginal populations, the looting of the conquered, and the 'commercial hunting of black skins' by the colonial system may all have been essential preconditions for what Marx called the 'primitive accumulation of capital'. These conditions are difficult to repeat today. Attitudes have changed – to no little extent because of Marx's own writings. Looting, slavery and colonialism now have no government's imprimatur. Most countries today are parties to treaties such as the Universal Declaration of Human Rights, and have constitutions which provide that equal access to property rights as one of the fundamental rights of humankind.

Moreover, as we saw in Chapter 6, authorities in developing countries have not been reticent in giving the poor access to assets. The bulk of spontaneous extralegal buildings and businesses in cities throughout the Second and Third Worlds may not have been formally titled, but governments have accepted (if only tacitly) their existence and ownership arrangements. In many developing countries during this century, large tracts of land have been given to poor farmers as part of agrarian reform programmes (though without the property representations necessary to create capital). Nor have authorities in those countries been reluctant to earmark budgets for property issues. Billions of dollars have been spent on activities related to registering ownership.

Property Makes Capital 'Mind Friendly'

Throughout this book I have been trying to demonstrate that we now have enough evidence to make substantial progress in development. With it in hand we can move beyond the stagnant 'left *v.* right' debate on property and avoid having to fight the same old battles all over again. Formal property is more than just ownership. As we saw in Chapter 3, it has to be viewed as the indispensable process that provides people with the tools to focus their thinking on those aspects of their resources from which they can extract capital. Formal property is more than a system for titling, recording and mapping assets – it is an instrument of thought, representing assets in such a way that people's minds can work on them to generate surplus value. That is why formal property must be universally accessible: to bring everyone into one social contract where they can cooperate to raise society's productivity.

What distinguishes a good legal property system is that it is 'mind friendly'. It obtains and organizes knowledge about recorded assets in forms we can control. It collects, integrates and coordinates not only data on assets and their potential, but our thoughts about them. In brief, capital results from the ability of the West to use property systems to represent their resources in a virtual context. Only there can minds meet to identify and realize assets' meaning for humankind.

The revolutionary contribution of an integrated property system is that it solves a basic problem of cognition. Our five senses are not sufficient for us to process the complex reality of an expanded market, much less a globalized one. We need to have the economic facts about ourselves and our resources boiled down to essentials that our minds can easily grasp. A good property system does that – it puts assets into a form that lets us distinguish their similarities, differences and connecting points with other assets. It fixes them in representations that the system tracks as they travel through time and space. In addition it allows assets to become fungible by representing them to our minds so that we can easily combine, divide and mobilize them to produce higher-valued mixtures. This capacity of property to represent aspects of assets in forms that allow us to recombine them so as to make them even more useful is the mainspring of economic growth, since growth is all about obtaining high-value outputs from low-value inputs.

A good legal property system is a medium that allows us to understand each other, make connections and synthesize knowledge about our assets to enhance our productivity. It is a way to represent reality that lets us transcend the limitations of our senses. Well-crafted property representations enable us to pinpoint the economic potential of resources so as to enhance what we can do with them. They are not 'mere paper': they are mediating devices that give us useful knowledge about things that are not manifestly present.

Property records point our knowledge about things towards an end, to borrow from Thomas Aquinas, 'just as the arrow is moved by the archer'.[12] By representing economic aspects of the things we own and assembling them into categories that our minds can quickly grasp, property documents reduce the costs of dealing with assets and increase their value commensurately. This notion, that the value of things can be increased by reducing the costs of knowing them and transacting with them, is one of Nobel laureate Ronald Coase's major contributions. In his treatise 'The Nature of the Firm' Coase established that the costs of carrying out transactions can be substantially reduced within the controlled and coordinated context of a firm.[13] In this sense property systems are like Coase's firm – controlled environments to reduce transaction costs.

The capacity of property to reveal the capital that is latent in the assets we accumulate is borne out of the best intellectual tradition of controlling our environment in order to prosper. For thousands of years our wisest men have been telling us that life has different degrees of reality, many of them invisible, and that it is only by constructing representational devices that we will be able to access them. In Plato's famous analogy we are likened to prisoners chained in a cave with our backs to the entrance so that all we can know of the world are the shadows cast on the wall in front of us. The truth that this illustration consecrates is that many things that guide our destiny are not self-evident. That is why civilization has worked hard to fashion representational systems to access and grasp that part of our reality that is virtual and represent it in terms we can understand.

As Margaret Boden puts it, 'Some of the most important human creations have been new representational systems. These include formal notations, such as Arabic numerals (not forgetting zero), chemical formulae, or the staves, minims and crotchets used by musicians. [Computer] programming languages are a more recent example.'[14] Representational systems such as mathematics and integrated property help us manipulate and order the complexities of the world in a manner that we can all understand and that allows us to communicate regarding issues that we could not otherwise handle. They are what the philosopher Daniel Dennett has called 'prosthetic extensions of the mind'.[15] Through representations we bring key aspects of the world into being so as to change the way we think about it. The philosopher John Searle has noted that by human agreement we can assign 'a new status to some phenomenon, where that status has an accompanying function that cannot be performed solely in virtue of the intrinsic physical features of the phenomenon in question'.[16] This seems to me very close to what legal property does: it assigns to assets, by social contract, in a conceptual universe, a status that allows them to perform functions that generate capital.

This notion that we organize reality in a conceptual universe is at the centre of philosophy worldwide. In France philosopher Michel Foucault labelled it the 'région médiane' that provides a system of switches (*codes fondamentaux)* that constitutes the secret network where society establishes the ever-expanding range of its potential (*les conditions de possibilité).*[17] I see formal property as a kind of switchyard that allows us to extend the potential of the assets that we accumulate further and further, each time increasing capital. I have also benefited from Karl Popper's notion of *World 3* – a separate reality from *World 1* of physical objects and *World 2* of mental states – where the products of our minds take on an autonomous existence that affects the way we deal with physical reality.[18] And it is to this conceptual world that formal property takes us – a world where the West organizes knowledge about assets and extracts from them the potential to generate capital.

And so formal property is this extraordinary thing, much bigger than simple ownership. Unlike tigers and wolves, who bare their teeth to protect their territory, man, physically a

much weaker animal, has used his mind to create a legal environment – property – to protect his territory. Without anyone
fully realizing it, the representational systems the West created
to settle territorial claims took on lives of their own, providing
the knowledge base and rules necessary to fix and realize
capital.

The Enemies of Representations

Ironically, the enemies of capitalism have always seemed more
aware of the virtual origin of capital than capitalists themselves. It is this virtual aspect of capitalism that they find so
insidious and dangerous. Capitalism, charges Viviane
Forrester in her bestseller *L'horreur économique*, 'has invaded
physical as well as virtual space . . . it has confiscated and
hidden wealth like never before, it has taken it out of the reach
of people by hiding it in the form of symbols. Symbols have
become the subjects of abstract exchanges that take place
nowhere else than in their virtual world.'[19] Consciously or
unconsciously, Forrester is part of a long tradition of being
uncomfortable with economic representations of virtual reality
– those 'metaphysical subtleties' that Marx thought were nevertheless necessary to understand and accumulate wealth.[20]

This fear of the virtuality of capital is understandable. Every
time civilization comes up with a novel way of using representations to manage the physical world people are suspicious.
When Marco Polo returned from China he shocked Europeans
with the news that the Chinese used not metal but paper
money, which people quickly denounced as alchemy. The
European world resisted representative money into the nineteenth century. The latest forms of derivative money –
electronic money, wire transfers and the now omnipresent
credit card – also took time to be accepted. As representations
of value become less ponderous and more virtual, people are
understandably sceptical. New forms of property derivatives

(such as mortgage-backed securities) may help form additional capital, but they also make understanding economic life more complex. And so people are inclined to be more comfortable with the image of the noble perspiring workers of Soviet and Latin American murals, toiling in the fields or operating their machines, than with capitalists wheeling and dealing titles, shares and bonds in the virtual reality of their computers. It is as if working with representations dirties your hands more than working with dirt and grease.

Like all representative systems – from written language to money and cyber symbols – property paper has been seen by many intellectuals as an instrument of deceit and oppression. Negative attitudes to representations have been powerful undercurrents in the formation of political ideas. The French philosopher Jacques Derrida recalls in *De la Grammatologie* how Jean Jacques Rousseau argued that writing was an important cause of human inequality. For Rousseau, those with the knowledge of writing could control written laws and official paper, and thus the destiny of people. Claude Lévi-Strauss has also argued that 'the primary function of written communication is to facilitate subjugation'.[21]

I am as aware as any anti-capitalist of how representational systems, particularly those of capitalism, have been used to exploit and conquer; how they have left the many at the mercy of the few. I have discussed in this book how official paper has been used for outright domination. And yet the art and science of representation is one of the girders of modern society. No amount of ranting and raving against writing, electronic money, cyber symbols and property paper will make them disappear. Instead we must make representational systems simpler and more transparent, and work hard to help people understand them. Otherwise, legal apartheid will persist and the tools to create wealth will remain in the hands of those who live inside the bell jar.

Is Succeeding at Capitalism a Cultural Thing?

Think of Bill Gates, the world's most successful and wealthiest entrepreneur. Apart from his personal genius, how much of his success is due to his cultural background and his 'Protestant Ethic'? And how much is due to the legal property system of the United States?

How many software innovations could he have made without patents to protect them? How many deals and long-term projects could he have carried out without enforceable contracts? How many risks could he have taken at the beginning without limited liability systems and insurance policies? How much capital could he have accumulated without property records in which to fix and store that capital? How many resources could he have pooled without fungible property representations? How many other people would he have made millionaires without being able to distribute stock options? How many economies of scale could he have benefited from if he had to operate on the basis of dispersed cottage industries that could not be combined? How would he pass on the rights to his empire to his children and colleagues without hereditary succession?

I do not think Bill Gates or any entrepreneur in the West could be successful without property rights systems based on a strong, well-integrated social contract. I humbly suggest that before any brahmin who lives in a bell jar tries to convince us that succeeding at capitalism requires certain cultural traits, we should first try to see what happens when developing and former communist countries establish property rights systems that can create capital for everyone.

Throughout history people have confused the efficiency of the representational tools they have inherited to create surplus value with the inherent values of their culture. They forget that often what gives an edge to a particular group of people is the innovative use they make of a representational system developed by another culture. For example, Northerners had to copy the legal institutions of ancient Rome to organize themselves, and learn the Greek alphabet and Arabic number symbols and systems to convey information and calculate. And so, today, few are aware of the tremendous edge that formal property systems have given Western societies. As a result, many Westerners have been led to believe that what underpins their successful capitalism is the work ethic they have inherited, or the existential anguish created by their religions – in spite of the fact that people all over the world all work hard when they can, and that existential angst or overbearing mothers are not Calvinist or Jewish monopolies. (I am as anxious as any Calvinist in history, especially on Sunday evenings, and in the overbearing mother sweepstakes, I would put mine in Peru up against any woman in New York.) Therefore, a great part of the research agenda needed to explain why capitalism fails outside the West remains mired in a mass of unexamined and largely untestable assumptions labelled 'culture', whose main effect is to allow too many of those who live in the privileged enclaves of this world to enjoy feeling superior.

One day these cultural arguments will peel away as the hard evidence of the effects of good political institutions and property law sink in. In the meantime, as *Foreign Affairs*' Fareed Zakaria has observed,

> Culture is hot. By culture I don't mean Wagner and Abstract Expressionism – they've always been hot – but rather culture as an explanation for social phenomena . . . Cultural explanations persist because intellectuals like them. They make valuable the detailed knowledge of countries' histories, which intellectuals have in great supply. They add an air of mystery and complexity to the study of societies . . . But culture itself can be shaped and changed. Behind so many cultural attitudes, tastes, and preferences lie the political and economic forces that shaped them.'[22]

This is not to say that culture does not count. All people in the world have specific preferences, skills and patterns of behaviour that can be regarded as cultural. The challenge is fathoming which of these traits are really the ingrained, unchangeable identity of a people and which are determined by economic and legal constraints. Is illegal squatting on real estate in Egypt and Peru the result of ancient, ineradicable nomadic traditions among the Arabs and the Quechuas' back-and-forth custom of cultivating crops at different vertical levels of the Andes? Or does it happen because in both Egypt and Peru it takes more than fifteen years to obtain legal property rights to desert land? In my experience squatting is mainly due to the latter. When people have access to an orderly mechanism to settle land that reflects the social contract, they will take the legal route and only a minority, like anywhere else, will insist on extralegal appropriation. Much behaviour that is today attributed to cultural heritage is not the inevitable result of people's ethnic or idiosyncratic traits but of their rational evaluation of the relative costs and benefits of entering the legal property system.

Legal property empowers individuals in any culture, and I doubt that property *per se* directly contradicts any major culture. Vietnamese, Cuban and Indian migrants have clearly had few problems adapting to US property law. If correctly conceived, property law can reach beyond cultures to increase trust between them and, at the same time, reduce the costs of bringing things and thoughts together.[23] Legal property sets the exchange rates between different cultures and thus gives them a bedrock of economic commonalities from which to do business with each other.

The Only Game in Town

I am convinced that capitalism has lost its way in developing and former communist nations. It is not equitable. It is out of touch with those who should be its largest constituency, and instead of being a cause that promises opportunity for all, capitalism appears increasingly as the leitmotif of a self-serving guild of businessmen and their technocracies. I hope this book has conveyed my belief that this state of affairs is relatively easy to correct —provided that governments are willing to accept the following:

1 the situation and potential of the poor need to be better documented;

2 all people are capable of saving;

3 what the poor are missing are the legally integrated property systems that can convert their work and savings into capital;

4 civil disobedience and the mafias of today are not marginal phenomena but the result of people marching by the billions from life organized on a small scale to life on a big scale;

5 in this context the poor are not the problem but the solution;

6 implementing a property system that creates capital is a political challenge because it involves getting in touch with people, grasping the social contract and overhauling the legal system.

With its victory over communism, capitalism's old agenda for economic progress is exhausted and requires a new set of commitments. It makes no sense continuing to call for open economies without facing the fact that the economic reforms under way open the doors only for small and globalized élites and leave out most of humanity. At present, capitalist globalization is concerned with interconnecting only the élites that live inside the bell jars. To lift the bell jars and do away with property apartheid will require going beyond the existing borders of both economics and law.

I am not a diehard capitalist. I do not view capitalism as a credo. Much more important to me are freedom, compassion for the poor, respect for the social contract and equal opportunity. But for the moment, to achieve those goals, capitalism is the only game in town. It is the only system we know that provides us with the tools required to create massive surplus value.

I love being from the Third World because it represents such a marvellous challenge – that of making a transition to a market-based capitalist system that respects people's desires and beliefs. When capital is a success story not only in the West but everywhere, we can move beyond the limits of the physical world and use our minds to soar into the future.

Many of the ideas in this book are based on practical research carried out in different countries in the world. If you would like to find out further information about the nature of this work, please refer to the Institute of Liberty and Democracy's website at:

www.ild.org.pe

APPENDIX

HOW MUCH DEAD CAPITAL ?

US$ 132,9 BILLION OF DEAD CAPITAL

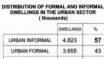

Owned by 65% of the population

Dead Capital	US$ Billion
Urban	
Metro Manila and adjacent areas	66,4
Informal Metro Manila	21,3
Previously formal areas	39,8
Adjacent areas	5,3
Other cities of the Philippines	5,7
Total	**72,1**
Rural	
Non alienable and disposable lands	40,8
Untitled alienable and disposable lands	6,3
Titled alienabled and disposable lands with restrictions	13,7
Total	**60,8**
US$ 132,9 Billion	

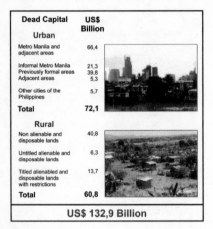

43%

Urban Informal 57%

DISTRIBUTION OF FORMAL AND INFORMAL DWELLINGS IN THE URBAN SECTOR
(thousands)

	DWELLINGS	%
URBAN INFORMAL	4.823	**57**
URBAN FORMAL	3.655	43
TOTAL URBAN	8.478	100

33%

Rural Informal 67%

DISTRIBUTION OF FORMAL AND INFORMAL AREAS IN THE RURAL SECTOR
(thousands)

	HECTARES	%
RURAL INFORMAL	20.623	**67**
RURAL FORMAL	10.077	33
TOTAL RURAL	30.700	100

Another way of saying this is that US$ 132,9 billion of informal capital is:

4 times greater than the market value of the 216 domestic companies listed in the Philippine Stock Exchange (US$ 31,4 billion) at the end of 1997.

5 times greater than the value of total mineral production (US$ 23,6 billion) in the last 20 years 1979 - 1998.

7 times greater than total savings and time deposits in commercial banks in the Philippines (US$18,8 billion) as of October 1998.

9 times greater than the capital of the largest state-owned enterprises in the Philippines at the end of 1998 (US$ 14,3 billion).

14 times greater than the value of total foreign direct investment in the Philippines (US$ 9,6 billion) between 1973 and September 1998.

Figure A.1
Philippines (Population : 68 million)

HOW MUCH DEAD CAPITAL ?

US$ 74,2 BILLION OF DEAD CAPITAL

Owned by 65%
of the population

Dead Capital	US$ Billion	
Urban		
Metropolitan Lima	18,5	
Other cities	18,0	
Total	**36,5**	
		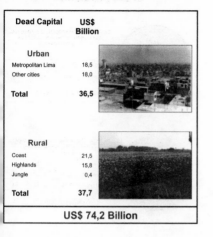
Rural		
Coast	21,5	
Highlands	15,8	
Jungle	0,4	
Total	**37,7**	
US$ 74,2 Billion		

47%

Urban Informal 53%

DISTRIBUTION OF FORMAL AND INFORMAL DWELLINGS IN THE URBAN SECTOR (thousands)

	DWELLINGS	%
URBAN INFORMAL	1.700	**53**
URBAN FORMAL	1.500	47
TOTAL URBAN	3.200	100

19%

Rural Informal 81%

DISTRIBUTION OF FORMAL AND INFORMAL AREAS IN THE RURAL SECTOR (thousands)

	HOLDINGS	%
RURAL INFORMAL	4.400	**81**
RURAL FORMAL	1.000	19
TOTAL RURAL	5.400	100

Another way of saying this is that
US$ 74,2 billion of informal capital is:

2 times greater than the total market value of the private companies registered in the stock exchange, 1995

2 times greater than the total assets of the 1,000 largest private formal enterprises

8 times greater than the total savings and time deposits in commercial banks in Peru, 1995

11 times greater than the capital of the largest public enterprises in Peru that could be freed through privatization

14 times greater than the value of direct foreign investment in Peru up to 1995

Figure A.2
Perú (Population : 24 million)

HOW MUCH DEAD CAPITAL ?

US$ 5,2 BILLION OF DEAD CAPITAL

Owned by 82% of the population

Dead Capital	US$ Billion
Urban	
Port-Au-Prince	1,8
Other cities	0,2
Total	**2,0**
Rural	
Total	**3,2**
US$ 5,2 Billion	

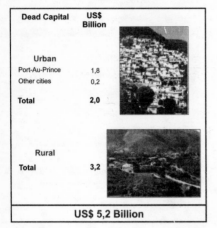

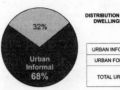

DISTRIBUTION OF FORMAL AND INFORMAL DWELLINGS IN THE URBAN SECTOR
(thousands)

	DWELLINGS	%
URBAN INFORMAL	349	**68**
URBAN FORMAL	163	32
TOTAL URBAN	512	100

DISTRIBUTION OF FORMAL AND INFORMAL AREAS IN THE RURAL SECTOR
(thousands)

	HECTARES	%
RURAL INFORMAL	1.527	**97**
RURAL FORMAL	41	3
TOTAL RURAL	1.568	100

Another way of saying this is that US$ 5,2 billion of informal capital is:

4 times greater than the total assets of the 123 largest private formal enterprises

9 times greater than the capital of the largest public enterprises in Haiti that could be freed through privatization

11 times greater than the total savings and time deposits in commercial banks in Haiti, 1995

158 times greater than the value of direct foreign investment in Haiti up to 1995

Figure A.3
Haiti (Population : 7 million)

HOW MUCH DEAD CAPITAL ?

S$ 241,4 BILLION OF DEAD CAPITAL

Owned by 85% of the population

Dead Capital	US$ Billion
Urban	
Greater Cairo	79,4
Alexandria	23,1
Other cities	51,8
Residential rural	40,9
Total	**195,2**
Rural	
Lower Egypt	28,1
Upper Egypt	18,1
Total	**46,2**

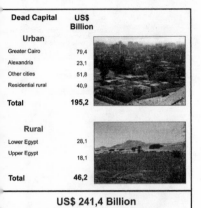

US$ 241,4 Billion

8%

Urban Informal 92%

DISTRIBUTION OF FORMAL AND INFORMAL DWELLINGS IN THE URBAN SECTOR (million)

	DWELLINGS	%
URBAN INFORMAL	11,9	92
URBAN FORMAL	1,0	8
TOTAL URBAN	12,9	100

17%

Rural Informal 83%

DISTRIBUTION OF FORMAL AND INFORMAL HOLDINGS IN THE RURAL SECTOR (million)

	HOLDINGS	%
RURAL INFORMAL	2,4	83
RURAL FORMAL	0,5	17
TOTAL RURAL	2,9	100

Another way of saying this is that US$ 241,4 billion of informal capital is:

6 times greater than total savings and time deposits in commercial banks in Egypt.

13 times greater than accumulated net foreign reserves up to 1996.

16 times greater than accumulated investment in formal assets made by private firms attracted by incentives given by the government of Egypt through the Investment Law.

30 times greater than the market value of the 746 companies that registered in the Cairo Stock Exchange in response to incentives provided by the Capital Market Law.

55 times greater than the value of direct foreign investment in Egypt up to 1996.

116 times greater than the value of the 63 public enterprises privatized between 1992 and 1996

Figure A.4
Egypt (Population : 63 million)

Typology 1
Average value: US$ 500

Typology 2
Average value: US$ 3,000

Typology 3
Average value: US$ 8,000

Typology 4
Average value: US$12,000

Typology 5
Average value: US$22,000

Typology 7
Average value: US$75,000

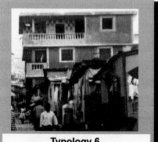

Typology 6
Average value: US$35,000

Figure A.5
Types of Urban Informality
in Port-Au-Prince and other
Haitian Cities

NOTES

Chapter 1
1 Gordon S. Wood, 'Inventing American Capitalism', *New York Review of Books*, 9 June 1994, p. 49.

Chapter 2
1 Donald Pisani, *Water, Land, and Law in the West: The Limits of Public Policy, 1850–1920* (Lawrence: University Press of Kansas, 1996), p. 51.
2 Comments by the architect and urbanist Albert Mangonese in *Conjonction*, No. 119, February–March 1973, p. 11.
3 Leonard J. Rolfes, Jr, 'The Struggle for Private Land Rights in Russia', *Economic Reform Today*, No. 1, 1996, p. 12.

Chapter 3
1 Adam Smith, *The Wealth of Nations* (London: Everyman's Library, 1977), former Vol. I, p. 242.
2 Ibid., p. 295.
3 Simonde de Sismondi, *Nouveaux principes d'économic politique* (Paris: Calmann-Lévy, 1827), pp. 81–2.
4 Jean Baptiste Say, *Traité d'économie politique* (Paris: Deterville, 1819), Vol. II, p. 429.
5 Karl Marx, Frederick Engels, *Collected Works* (New York: International Publishers, 1996), Vol. XXXV, p. 82.
6 Smith, *The Wealth of Nations,* former Vol. I, p. 242.
7 Ibid., p. 286.

8 Herbert L. Dreyfus and Paul Rabinow, *Michel Foucault: Beyond Structuralism and Hermeneutics* (Chicago: Harvester, University of Chicago, 1982), p. 211.

9 George A. Miller and Philip N. Johnson-Laird, *Language and Perception* (Cambridge, MA: Harvard University Press, 1976), p. 578.

10 Gunnar Heinsohn and Otto Steiger, 'The Property Theory of Interest and Money', unpublished manuscript, second draft, October 1998, p. 22.

11 Ibid., p. 43.

12 Ibid., p. 38.

13 Tom Bethell, *The Noblest Triumph*, (New York: St Martin's Press, 1998), p. 9.

14 Fernand Braudel, *The Wheels of Commerce* (New York: Harper and Row, 1982), p. 248.

Chapter 4

1 'Survey the Internet', *The Economist*, 1 July 1995, pp. 4–5.

2 Jeb Blount, 'Latin Trade', *News Finance*, 20 January 1997.

3 Tony Emerson and Michael Laris, 'Migration', *Newsweek*, 4 December 1995.

4 Henry Boldrick, 'Reaching Turkey's Spontaneous Settlements', *World Bank Policy*, April–June 1996.

5 'Solving the Squatter Problem', *Business World*, 10 May 1995.

6 *Newsweek*, 23 March 1998.

7 *The Economist*, 6 June 1998.

8 Manal El-Batran and Ahmed El-Kholei, *Gender and Rehousing in Egypt* (Cairo: The Royal Netherlands Embassy in Cairo, 1996), p. 24.

9 Gerard Barthelemy, 'L'extension des lotissements sauvages à usage populaire en milieu urbain ou Paysans, Villes et Bidonvilles en Haiti: Aperçus et reflexions', Port-au-Prince, offprint, June 1996.

10 Blount, 'Latin Trade'.

11 Rolfes, 'The Struggle for Private Land Rights in Russia'.

12 Official journal of the *National Geographic Society* (Millennium in Maps), No. 4, October 1998.

13 Donald Stewart, *AIPE*, December 1997.

14 Matt Moffett, 'The Amazon Jungle Had an Eager Buyer, But Was It For Sale?', *The Wall Street Journal*, 30 January 1997.

15 Simon Fass, *Political Economy in Haiti: The Drama of Survival* (New Brunswick, NJ: Transaction Publishers, 1988), pp. xxiv–xxv.

16 Ahmed M. Soliman, 'Legitimizing informal housing: accommodating low-income groups in Alexandria, Egypt', *Environment and Urbanization*, Vol. 8, No. 1, April 1996, pp. 190–1.

17 Reuters, printed in *Financial Review*, 11 May 1992, p. 45.

18 Mavery Zarembo, *Newsweek*, 7 July 1997.

19 *The Economist*, 5 March 1994.

20 Ibid., 6 May 1995.

21 'Terrenos de Gamarra valen tres veces más que en el centro de Lima', *El Comercio*, 25 April 1995.

22 Jan De Vries, *Economy of Europe in an Age of Crisis, 1600–1750* (Cambridge: Cambridge University Press, 1976); D.C. Coleman, *Revisions in Mercantilism* (London: Methuen and Co., Ltd, 1969); J.H. Clapham, *The Economic Development of France and Germany, 1815–1914* (Cambridge: Cambridge University Press, 1963); Eli Heckscher, *Mercantilism*, ed. E.F. Soderland (London: Allen & Unwin, 1934).

23 Joseph Reid, *Respuestas al primer cuestionario del ILD* (Lima: Meca, 1985).

24 D.C. Coleman, *The Economy of England 1450–1750* (Oxford: Oxford University Press, 1977), pp. 18–19.

25 Ibid., pp. 58–9.

26 Heckscher, *Mercantilism*, vol. 1, p. 323.

27 Ibid., p. 241.

28 Robert B. Ekelund, Jr. and Robert Tollison, *Mercantilism as a Rent Seeking Society* (College Station: Texas A&M University Press, 1981), Chapter 1.

29 Heckscher, *Mercantilism*, Vol. 1, pp. 239–44.

30 Coleman, *The Economy of England*, p. 74.

31 Heckscher, *Mercantilism*, Vol. 1, p. 244.

32 Clapham, *Economic Development of France and Germany*, pp. 323–5.

33 Joseph Reid responds to the second questionnaire submitted by the ILD, typewritten memoranda, ILD Library, 1985; Heckscher, *Mercantilism*, Vol. 1, pp. 247, 251.

34 Charles Wilson, *Mercantilism* (London: Routledge & Kegan Paul, 1963), p. 27.

35 Coleman, *The Economy of England*, p. 105.

Chapter 5

1 Francis S. Philbrick, 'Changing Conceptions of Property Law',' *University of Pennsylvania Law Review*, Vol. 86, May 1938, p. 691.

2 Bernard Bailyn, *The Peopling of British North America: An Introduction* (New York: Knopf, 1986), p. 5.

3 Peter Charles Hoffer, *Law and People in Colonial America* (Baltimore: Johns Hopkins University Press, 1998), pp. 1–2.

4 Ibid., p. xii.

5 David Thomas Konig, 'Community Custom and the Common Law: Social Change and the Development of Land Law in Seventeenth-century Massachusetts', in *Land Law and Real Property in American History: Major Historical Interpretations*, ed. Kermit Hall (New York: Garland Publishing, 1987), p. 339.

6 Ibid., pp. 319–20.

7 Ibid., p. 320.

8 Ibid., p. 323.

9 Ibid., p. 324.

10 Ibid., p. 349.

11 Hoffer, *Law and People in Colonial America*, p. 15.

12 Amelia C. Ford, *Colonial Precedents of our National Land System as it Existed in 1800* (Philadelphia: Porcupine Press, 1910) pp. 112–13.

13 Ibid., p. 114.

14 Konig, 'Community Custom', p. 325.

15 Ibid., p. 325.

16 Aaron Morton Sokolski, *Land Tenure and Land Taxation in America* (New York: Schalkenbach Foundation, 1957), p. 191.

17 Ibid., p. 191.

18 Henry W. Tatter, *The Preferential Treatment of the Actual Settler in the Primary Disposition of the Vacant Lands in the United States to 1841*, Ph.D. dissertation, Northwestern University, 1933, Tatter, *The Preferential Treatment*, p. 273.

19 Ibid., p. 23.

20 Ford, *Colonial Precedents*, p. 103.

21 Ibid., p. 103.

22 Ibid., pp. 89–90.

23 Ibid., p.126.

24 Ibid., p. 126.

25 Ibid., p. 128.

26 Ibid., p. 129.

27 Ibid., p. 130.

28 Tatter, *The Preferential Treatment*, pp. 40–1.

29 Quoted in Stanley Lebergott, "O'Pioneers": Land Speculation and the Growth of the Midwest', in *Essays on the Economy of the Old*

Northwest, ed. David C. Klingman and Richard K. Vedder (Athens, OH: Ohio University Press, 1987), p. 39.

30 Ford, *Colonial Precedents*, p. 119.

31 Sokolski, *Land Tenure*, p. 192.

32 Ibid., p. 193.

33 Ibid.

34 Quoted in Pisani, *Water, Land, and Law*, p. 51.

35 Sokolski, *Land Tenure*, pp. 193–4.

36 Lebergott, '"O'Pioneers"', pp. 39–40.

37 Ibid.

38 Ibid., p. 40.

39 Act XXXIII, March 1642, *The Statutes at Large, Being a Collection of all the Laws of Virginia from the First Session of the Legislature*, ed. William Henning (New York, 1823), p. 134.

40 Richard E. Messick, 'A History of Preemption Laws in the United States', *draft prepared for ILD*, p. 7.

41 Ford, *Colonial Precedents*, p. 124.

42 Ibid., p. 124.

43 Ibid., p. 132.

44 Ibid., p. 134.

45 An Act for Adjusting and Settling the Titles of Claimers to Unpatented Land under the Present and Former Government, Previous to the Establishment of the Commonwealth's Land Office, *The Statutes at Large: Being a Collection of all the Laws of Virginia*, ed. William Hening (Richmond, 1822), p. 40.

46 Douglas W. Allen, 'Homesteading and Property Rights; or "How the West was Really Won"', *Journal of Law & Economics* 34 (April 1991), p. 6.

47 Richard Current et al, Eds., *American History: A Survey*, 7th edition (New York: Knopf, 1987), p. 150.

48 Terry L. Anderson, 'The First Privatization Movement', in *Essays on the Economy of the Old Northwest*, p. 63.

49 Current, *American History*, p. 150.

50 Roy M. Robbins, 'Preemption – A Frontier Triumph', *Mississippi Valley Historical Review*, Vol. 18, December 1931, pp. 333–4.

51 Ibid.

52 Ford, *Colonial Precedents*, p. 117.

53 Lebergott, ' "O'Pioneers," ' p. 40.

54 Ibid., p. 40.

55 Messick, 'A History of Preemption', p. 9.

56 Quoted in Tatter, *The Preferential Treatment*, pp. 91–2.

57 Messick, 'A History of Preemption', p. 10.

58 Act of 18 May 1796, *Public and General Statutes Passed by the Congress of the United States of America: 1789 to 1827 Inclusive*, ed. Joseph Story (Boston, 1828).

59 Tatter, *The Preferential Treatment*, p. 118.

60 Quoted in ibid., p. 125.

61 Patricia Nelson Limerick, *The Legacy of Conquest: The Unbroken Past of the American West* (New York: W.W. Norton & Company, 1987), p. 59.

62 Ibid.

63 Ibid., p. 140.

64 Lebergott, '"O'Pioneers"', p. 44.

65 Ibid.

66 Ibid.

67 Richard E. Messick, 'Rights to Land and American Economic Development', *draft prepared for ILD*, p. 44.

68 Richard White, *It's Your Misfortune and None of My Own: A New History of the American West* (Norman: University of Oklahoma Press, 1991), p. 146.

69 Ibid.

70 Stephen Schwartz, *From West to East* (New York: The Free Press, 1998), pp. 105–10.

71 Quoted in Lebergott, '"O'Pioneers"', p. 40

72 Quoted in Anderson, 'The First Privatization Movement', p. 63.

73 Paul W. Gates, *Landlords and Tenants on the Prairie Frontier* (Ithaca: Cornell University Press, 1973), p. 13.

74 Ibid., p. 16.

75 Quoted in ibid.

76 Quoted in ibid., p. 24.

77 Lawrence M. Friedman, *A History of American Law*, 2nd edition (New York: Simon & Schuster, 1986), pp. 241–2.

78 Quoted in ibid., p. 242.

79 Ibid.

80 G. Edward White, *The American Judicial Tradition: Profiles of Leading Judges* (New York: Oxford University Press, 1976), p. 48.

81 Quoted in Ford, *Colonial Precedents*, p. 129 (my emphasis).

82 Gates, *Landlords and Tenants*, p. 27.

83 *Green v. Biddle*, 8 Wheaton 1 (1823).

84 Ibid., p. 33.

85 Ibid., p. 66.

86 Gates, *Landlords and Tenants*, p. 37.

87 Current, *American History*, p. 149.

88 Quoted in ibid., p. 31.

89 Quoted in ibid.

90 Tatter, *The Preferential Treatment,* p. 265.

91 Gates, *Landlords and Tenants*, p. 33.

92 *Bodley v. Gaither*, 19 Kentucky Reports 57, 58 (1825).

93 *M'Kinney v. Carrol*, 21 Kentucky Reports 96, 97 (1827).

94 White, *It's Your Misfortune*, p. 139.

95 Gates, *Landlords and Tenants*, p. 46; *Congressional Record*, 43 Congress, I Session, 1603 (18 February 1874).

96 Pisani, *Water, Land, and Law*, p. 63.

97 Tatter, *The Preferential Treatment*, p. 154.

98 Gates, *Landlords and Tenants*, p. 44.

99 Paul W. Gates, 'California's Embattled Settlers', *The California Historical Society Quarterly*, Vol. 41, June 1962, p. 115.

100 Messick, 'A History of Preemption', p. 17.

101 Quoted in ibid.

102 Ibid., p. 19.

103 Act of 29 May 1830, *Public Statutes at Large of the United States of America*, Vol. 4 (Boston, 1846).

104 Act of 4 September 1841, *Public Statutes at Large of the United States of America*, Vol. 5 (Boston: Charles C. Little and James Brown, 1845–1867).

105 Messick, 'A History of Preemption', p. 26.

106 Pisani, *Water, Land, and Law*, p. 69.

107 Allan G. Bogue, 'The Iowa Claim Clubs: Symbol and Substance', in *The Public Lands: Studies in the History of the Public Domain*, ed. Vernon Carstensen (Madison: University of Wisconsin Press, 1963), p. 47.

108 Pisani, *Water, Land, and Law*, p. 53.

109 Ibid., p. 63.

110 Bogue, 'The Iowa Claim Clubs', p. 51.

111 Ibid., p. 50.

112 Quoted in ibid., p. 52.

113 Tatter, *The Preferential Treatment*, p. 276.

114 Bogue, 'The Iowa Claim Clubs', p. 54.

115 White, *It's Your Misfortune*, p. 141.

116 Tatter, *The Preferential Treatment*, p. 280.

117 Terry Anderson and P.J. Hill, 'An American Experiment in Anarcho-capitalism: The Not So Wild West', *Journal of Libertarian Studies*, Vol. 3, 1979, p. 15.

118 Ibid.

119 Bogue, 'The Iowa Claim Clubs', p. 50.

120 Ibid., p. 51.

121 Quoted in ibid., p. 54.

122 White, *It's Your Misfortune*, p. 141.

123 Bogue, 'The Iowa Claim Clubs', p. 55.

124 Tatter, *The Preferential Treatment*, p. 273.

125 Ibid., p. 287.

126 John Q. Lacy, 'Historical Overview of the Mining Law: The Miners' Law Becomes Law', *The Mining Law of 1872* (Washington, DC: National Legal Center for the Public Interest, 1984), p. 17.

127 Robert W. Swenson, 'Sources and Evolution of American Mining Law', in *The American Law of Mining*, ed. Matthew Bender (New York: Rocky Mountain Mineral Law Foundation, 1960), p. 19.

128 Gates, 'California's Embattled Settlers', p. 100.

129 Harold Krent, 'Spontaneous Popular Sovereignty in the United States', *draft prepared for ILD*, p. 2.

130 Pisani, *Water, Land, and Law*, p. 52.

131 Limerick, *Legacy of Conquest*, p. 65; also see White, *It's Your Misfortune*, p. 147.

132 Pisani, *Water, Land, and Law*, p. 69.

133 Ibid.

134 Gates, 'California's Embattled Settlers', p. 100.

135 Ibid., pp. 22–6.

136 Lacy, 'Historical Overview of the Mining Law', p. 26.

137 Quoted in Charles Howard Shinn, *Mining Camps: A Study in American Frontier Government* (New York: Alfred A. Knopf, 1948), p. 107.

138 *Gore v. McBreyer*, 18 Cal. 582 (1861), quoted in Lacy, 'Historical Overview of the Mining Law', p. 22.

139 Ibid., p. 21.

140 Ibid., pp. 24–5.

141 Swenson, 'Sources and Evolution', p. 24.

142 Ibid., p. 29.

143 Ibid., p. 30.

144 Ibid.

145 Krent, 'Spontaneous Popular Sovereignty', p. 3.

146 Lacy, 'Historical Overview of the Mining Law', p. 35.

147 14 Stat. 252 (1866).

148 Swenson, 'Sources and Evolution'.

149 Lacy, 'Historical Overview of the Mining Law,' p. 36.
150 Quoted in Krent, 'Spontaneous Popular Sovereignty', p. 3.
151 Lacy, 'Historical Overview of the Mining Law', pp. 37–8; 17 Stat. 91, 30 USC §§ 22–42
152 *Jennison v. Kirk*, 98 U.S. 240, 243 (1878).
153 Swenson, 'Sources and Evolution', p. 27.
154 Messick, 'Rights to Land and American Development'. p. 45.
155 White, *It's Your Misfortune*, p. 143.
156 Ibid., p. 145.
157 Wood, 'Inventing American Capitalism', p. 49.
158 White, *It's Your Misfortune*, p. 270.
159 White, *The American Judicial Tradition*, pp. 48–9.
160 Philbrick, 'Changing Conceptions', p. 694.

Chapter 6

1 C. Reinold Noyes, *The Institution of Property* (New York: Longman's Green, 1936), pp. 2 and 13.
2 For a very lucid and current discussion on this subject, see William M. Landes and Richard A. Posner, 'Adjudication as a Private Good', *Journal of Legal Studies*, Vol. 8, March 1979, pp. 235–84.
3 Noyes, *The Institution of Property*, p. 20.
4 John C. Payne, 'In Search of Title', Part 1, *Alabama Law Review*, Vol. 14, No. 1, 1961, p. 17.
5 Andrzej Rapaczynski, 'The Roles of the State and the Market in Establishing Property Rights', *Journal of Economic Perspectives*, Vol. 10, No. 2, Spring 1996, p. 88.
6 See Robert C. Ellickson, *Order without Law: How Neighbors Settle Disputes* (Cambridge, MA: Harvard University Press, 1991) for a most interesting discussion of how extralegal regulation governs property relationships in the United States.
7 See Richard A. Posner, 'Hegel and Employment at Will: A Comment', *Cardozo Law Review*, Vol. 10, March/April 1989.
8 Harold J. Berman, *Law and Revolution. The Formation of the Western Legal Tradition* (Cambridge, MA: Harvard University Press, 1983), pp. 555–6.
9 Ibid., p. 557.
10 Robert Cooter and Thomas Ulen, *Law and Economics, an Economic Theory of Property* (Reading, MA: Addison-Wesley, 1997), p. 79.
11 Margaret Gruter, *Law and the Mind* (London: Sage, 1991), p. 62.
12 Bruce L. Benson, *The Enterprise of Law* (San Francisco: Pacific

Research Institute for Public Policy, 1990), p. 2.

13 For an account of how informal organizations try to graduate into the formal sector see Hernando de Soto, *The Other Path: The Invisible Revolution in the Third World* (New York: Harper & Row, 1989), especially Chs 1–4.

14 Bruno Leoni, *Freedom and the Law* (Los Angeles: Nash Publishing, 1972), pp. 10–11.

15 See Robert Sugden, 'Spontaneous Order', *Journal of Economic Perspectives*, Vol. 3, No. 4, Fall 1989, especially pp. 93–4. Also see F.A. Hayek, *Law, Legislation and Liberty*, Vols I–III (London: Routledge & Kegan Paul Ltd, 1973).

16 Payne, 'In Search of Title', p. 20.

17 See John P. Powelson, *The Story of Land* (Cambridge, MA: Lincoln Institute of Land Policy, 1988).

18 Richard Pipes, *The Russian Revolution* (New York: Vintage Books, 1991), p. 112.

19 Samar K. Datta and Jeffrey B. Nugent, 'Adversary Activities and Per Capita Income Growth', *World Development*, Vol. 14, No. 12, 1986, p. 1458.

20 S. Rowton Simpson, *Land, Law and Registration* (Cambridge: Cambridge University Press, 1976), p. 170.

21 Peter Stein, *Legal Evolution: The Story of an Idea* (Cambridge: Cambridge University Press, 1980), p. 53.

22 Ibid., p. 55.

23 Lynn Holstein, 'Review of Bank Experience with Land Titling and Registration', working papers, March 1993, p. 9.

24 J.D. McLaughlin and S.E. Nichols, 'Resource Management: The Land Administration and Cadastral Systems Component', *Surveying and Mapping*, Vol. 49, No. 2, 1989, p. 84.

Chapter 7

1 Lester Thurow, *The Future of Capitalism* (New York: Penguin Books, 1996), p. 5.

2 Hernando de Soto, *The Other Path*.

3 'Side Effects of Egypt's Economic Reform Warned', *Xinhua* (CNN), 4 February 1999.

4 George F. Will, *The Pursuit of Virtue and Other Tory Notions* (New York: Simon & Schuster, 1982).

5 Klaus Schwab and Claude Smadja, 'Globalization Needs a Human Face', *International Herald Tribune*, 28 January 1999.

6 Tim Padgett, *Newsweek*, 16 September 1996.

7 George Soros, *The Crisis of Global Capitalism: Open Society Endangered* (New York: Public Affairs, 1998), p. xxvii.
8 Eugene Kamenka, ed., *The Portable Marx* (New York: Viking Penguin, 1993), p. 463.
9 Nancy Birdsall and Juan Luis Londoño, 'Assets in Equality Matters', *American Economic Review*, May 1997.
10 Kamenka, ed., *The Portable Marx*, p. 447.
11 Karl Marx, 'Capital', *Collected Works*, Vol. XXVIII, p. 235.
12 Thomas of Aquinas, *Summa Theologica*, Part I of Second Part Q.12, Art. 4 (London: Encyclopaedia Britannica, 1952), p. 672.
13 Ronald H. Coase, 'The Nature of the Firm', *Economica*, November 1937.
14 Margaret Boden, *The Creative Mind* (London: Abacus, 1992), p. 94.
15 Daniel C. Dennett, 'Intentionality', in *The Oxford Companion to the Mind*, ed. Richard L. Gregory (Oxford: Oxford University Press, 1991), p. 384.
16 John R. Searle, *The Construction of Social Reality* (New York: The Free Press, 1995), p. 46.
17 See Michel Foucault, *Les Mots et les choses* (Saint Amand: Gallimond, 1993).
18 Karl Popper, *Knowledge and the Body–Mind Problem* (London: Routledge, 1994).
19 Viviane Forrester, *L'horreur économique* (Paris: Fayard, 1996), p. 61 (my translation).
20 Karl Marx in Kamenka, ed., *The Portable Marx*, pp. 444–7.
21 Claude Lévi-Strauss, *Tristes Tropiques* (Paris: Plon, Terre Humaine/Poche, 1996), p. 354.
22 Fareed Zakaria, 'The Politics of Port', *Slate Magazine*, Internet, 16 March 1999.
23 Crucial reading regarding the phenomenon of trust and social cooperation is, of course, Francis Fukuyama's *Trust* (New York: The Free Press, 1995).

Acknowledgements

No one ever writes a book alone. I have benefited from the information, opinions, encouragement and support of many people – so many, in fact, that it is impossible to thank them all individually. But there are several without whom this book would never have come to be what it is, and I would like to register my gratitude in print.

First, there are my colleagues from the Institute of Liberty and Democracy (ILD) in Lima, Peru, who have been my constant companions in our quest to create a non-discriminatory market system where the law helps everyone to have an opportunity to prosper. The ideas in this book are backed up by the facts and figures uncovered by my ILD team in the field in our projects throughout the world. I truly stand on their shoulders. Manuel Mayorga La Torre, my chief operating officer, applied his long experience as a power plant project engineer to planning and organizing all our projects, day to day, right down the critical path. Luis Morales Bayro is the ILD's top economist, supervising the research and cost-benefit analysis in the countries in which we work. His work is crucial to our success in identifying the hidden costs of laws and institutions. Luis is assisted by Mario Galantini and backed up, when necessary, by Vittorio Corvo.

On the legal side are my two trusted and beloved colleagues

of the past fifteen years: Ana Lucia Camaiora manages ILD's legal teams and is responsible for bringing together the whole legal picture. She is closely supported by Maria del Carmen Delgado, our top legal analyst. They possess the sharpest minds in legal pluralism that I know. Not only do they understand the law but also its implications. Their efforts are supported by many other ILD lawyers, the principal heroes amongst whom, for the purpose of this book, are Gustavo Marini, Jackeline Silva, Luis Aliaga, and Guillermo Garcia Montufar. Our chief techie is Daniel Herencia, whose team, including Javier Robles and David Castillo, set up our computer systems in the field. Elsa Jo runs the administration of ILD, ably assisted by her chief accountant Eliana Silva and the rest of her staff.

Second, there are those who provided the intellectual subsoil that allowed me to process the information I obtained. No one has been closer to me during the saga of writing this book than Duncan Macdonald, my old friend and cosmic guide from Scotland. It was Duncan who introduced me to cognitive science, especially to the research being carried out in the theory of mind. To my delight, I was able to use what I read to analyse the results of my work in the field. I had already learned from the American anthropologist Douglas Uzzell about the usefulness in my work of the anthropologist's skill of 'participatory observation', and Georgetown law professor Warren Schwartz had taught me to apply economic principles to the analysis of law. But it was Duncan who showed me how philosophers of mind could help me to capture the connections I had been searching for between property and development. Our discussions about how humans can transform their environments into an extension of their minds were crucial to my understanding of how modern capital is created. When I was confused, stuck in an intellectual corner, or just plain in the dark, Duncan saved me.

I also wish to thank the German philosopher Dorothee Kreuzer for leading me through the subtleties of the French post-structuralists, particularly Jacques Derrida and Michel Foucault. From Derrida I learned that you can use categories from one culture to describe another in a way that everyone can understand – without violating the culture's unique character. And thus I was better able to understand how we were successfully integrating extralegal property arrangements into formal property law. From Foucault I learned the basics of the 'secret architecture' that links the invisible to the visible, also inferring from his writings how a good system of representations increases *la condition de possibilité* of all mankind. My sense of the economic power and significance of representations was increased even further by my reading in semiotics, principally Umberto Eco and Ferdinand de Saussure, and in philosophy of mind, particularly the work of John Searle and Daniel Dennett.

But it is my friend and colleague Mariano Cornejo who ensures that my ideas pass the severe test of landfall. No matter how ingenious or elegant an idea might be, it will not be allowed into an ILD project unless it passes Mariano's two primary requirements: that it works, and that it can be applied by very ordinary people. When I am right, he simply smiles and tells me I have stumbled over the obvious (*'No es problema, no es problema'*); when I am wrong, he points me in the right direction.

Then there are those without whose inspiration, encouragement and support I would not have been in the position to write this book. After twelve years of partnership, Stephan Schmidheiny has become a dear friend. An intellectual and philanthropist, as well as an extremely successful businessman, Stephan has contributed in many ways to the ILD's success. He has reinforced our efforts to find ways of giving opportunity to those who have been unjustly deprived of it. He has also fortified our belief that global markets without global laws are dangerous. But the principal way in which Stephan has influenced the ILD's work is by insisting on the need for realism: If idealism is not businesslike, ideals remain no more than ideals and of no use to those we have set out to help. Another very important and dear friend is Lawrence Chickering, a brilliant intellectual from San Francisco, who has helped the ILD to initiate many projects and adventures of the mind while continually helping me personally with his compassionate 'pastoral' counselling.

I could not forget my friends at the Agency for International Development: Brian Atwood, Dick McCall, Jim Michels, Norma Parker, Aaron Williams, Paula Goddard, and especially the terrific people at the Latin American and Caribbean Department, Mark Schneider, Carl Leonard, Michael Deal, Timothy Mahoney, William B. Baucom, Donald Drga, and Jolyne Sanjak. They not only provided the ILD with their support and encouragement throughout the years but also created many opportunities for us. And when I ran into an organizational problem my old friend John Sullivan, who directs the Center for International Private Enterprise, explained to me how US institutions would tackle it. He also taught me how the right set of institutions could turn conflicting positions into workable and profitable solutions. From my friend Bob Litan, of the Brookings Institution, I learned not only how law affects economic behaviour but also that there are valuable lessons for the rest of the world in how the financial revolution in the United States has increased capital formation. One June day in 1999 Bob walked into my house in Lima and said, 'I've got a great title for your book – *The Mystery of Capital*.' For that, too, I thank him.

Special thanks are due to the Smith Richardson Foundation, which supported much of the work done for this book in the form of a generous grant. The foundation is an old and loyal friend which, during the early Nineties when the ILD was being bombed and shot at, provided us with a bullet-proof vehicle, thus enabling us to continue with our work.

I am also most grateful to Harold Krent, Saul Levmore, Rick Messick, Tom Romero, and Larry Stay for their Herculean efforts in researching the history of US property. My gratitude also goes to my friends at Her Majesty's Land Registry in London – especially John Manthorpe and Christopher West – for pointing me to the books that helped me to understand the evolution of British property. Monika Bergmeier and Klaus Joachim Grigoleit helped me to investigate the origins of German property, and Hans-Urs Wili introduced me to the origins of Swiss property, instructing me on the conversion of Roman law in the Swiss and German traditions from a rigid system of rules to a more people-friendly one. Peter Schaeffer, my friend in Washington, DC, has contributed his thoughts, notes and observations, introducing me to others with valuable insights for our work.

Merran Van Der Tak helped me to explore the relationship between property rights and the development of public utilities. Oscar Beasley taught me how title insurance and securitization of real estate assets work. Robert Freedman deepened my shallow knowledge of Marxism. Lee and Alexandra Benham were extremely helpful in revising an early draft of this book.

This book also benefited from the invitations issued by various governments and non-governmental organizations to design and implement projects in their own countries aimed at capitalizing the poor. The opportunity to collect information, analyse institutions and legislation, and to interview participants in both the legal and underground sectors on virtually every continent helped me to make this book relevant to most of the countries in the world. At this stage I can publicly thank associates in only three of the countries in which we are currently. In Egypt I am indebted to my friends and counterparts at the Egyptian Centre for Economic Studies, Ahmed Galal, Hisham Fahmy, Taher Helmy, Gamal Mubarak and their staff. Sherif El Diwany has been instrumental throughout to the ILD's work in Egypt. Also crucial was the support of Prime Minister Atef Ebeid, Minister of Finance Medhat Hassanein, Minister of the Economy Yousef Boutros Ghali, and Minister of Social Affairs Mervat El Talawi. In Haiti, I am grateful for the continual support of President Rene Preval and former President Jean Bertrand Aristide and their staffs. I am also indebted to the Centre pour la Libre Enterprise et la Democratie, particularly Georges Sassine, Lionel Delatour, Bernard Craan and Jean Maurice Buteau. In the Philippines, the aid we received from President Joseph Estrada and Executive Secretary Ronaldo Zamora was crucial for our progress. Our research has been completed thanks to the efforts and support of Vic Taylor, along with Ernesto Garilao, Jose P. Leviste, Arturo Alvendia, Alex Melchor and many others.

The manuscript of this book would never have seen the light of day without Iris MacKenzie, who guided my English through countless drafts; as my first reader and copy editor Iris constantly directed me towards clarity. I want to thank my assistant Miriam Gago for helping us to make the manuscript fit for the eyes of publishers throughout the world. But, most important, it was her efficient supervision of my life and paperwork that allowed me to spend great chunks of time away from the office writing this book.

Finally, I want to extend my gratitude to several people who helped me turn a few good ideas into a book. My agent Andrew Wylie has been a shrewd source of wisdom in how to make a book come alive for an international audience. He set a high standard and never permitted me to fall short of it. Once I had a manuscript, my friends David Frum and Mirko Lauer became its architects; in ten days, they took the existing draft, turned it upside down, and, in Frum's phrase, 'pressed the water out of it', shaping it into its current structure. To ready the final manuscript for meeting potential publishers I was fortunate to have Edward Tivnan on my side. A journalist and author whose doctorate in philosophy makes him as comfortable with ideas as he is with deadlines, Tivnan spent fifty days with me in Lima, rewriting the entire book, sentence by sentence.

Bill Frucht, my US editor, did a magnificent job of preparing the book for publication, helping me to clarify many points and thus improving the book immensely. Sally Gaminara was my British editor. Her editorial talent was superseded only by her ingenuity and creativity for publishing and promoting this book.

The success of the final product is due to all of the above. Its limitations are mine.

INDEX